Heaven's SUCCESS SECRETS

12 KEYS TO LIVING THE LIFE
YOU WERE MADE TO ENJOY

Heaven's SUCCESS SECRETS

EUGENE H. LOWE, PH.D.

Oviedo, Florida

Heaven's Success Secrets—12 Keys to Living the Life You Were Made to Enjoy by Eugene H. Lowe, Ph.D.

Published by HigherLife Development Services, Inc.
400 Fontana Circle
Building 1 Suite 105
Oviedo, Florida 32765
(407) 563-4806
www.ahigherlife.com

All scripture is taken from the New American Standard Bible®, copyright © The Lockman Foundation 1960, 1962, 1963, 1968, 1971, 1972, 1973, 1975, 1977, 1995. Used by permission. (www. Lockman.org)

ISBN 13: 978-1-935245-23-0
ISBN 10: 1-935245-23-6

Cover Design: Judith McKittrick Wright

First Edition

10 11 12 13 — 9 8 7 6 5 4 3 2 1

Printed in the United States of America

This book is dedicated to everyone who seeks more real successes in life.

TABLE OF CONTENTS

ACKNOWLEDGMENTS

Much of my free time for four years was consumed with writing, editing, and re-editing the manuscript for this book. The inspiration and insights that I experienced were a great joy to me.

I thank my wife Brenda whom I love more than life itself for her encouragement, help, and counsel, and for unselfishly allowing me the time for writing this book.

I am grateful for my friends the Reverend Claude Smithmier, E.J. "Woody" Clark, and Eric Forsgren, who provided me with insightful feedback on an early draft.

I thank Dave Welday, who worked with me to turn the manuscript into a published book, and Deborah Poulalion, who edited the manuscript.

Finally, I thank my many other friends who encouraged me along the way.

INTRODUCTION

I have wonderful news: God wants us to be successful! He wants us to be successful in our personal lives. He wants us to be successful in our relationships. He wants us to be successful in our businesses and our careers. His plan for us includes those areas and more. His plan is a good plan. It is a practical plan. It is an individualized plan. It is an achievable plan as we cooperate with him. It is a plan to develop and bless us. God declared his intention through the prophet Jeremiah:

> "For I know the plans that I have for you," declares the Lord, "plans for welfare and not for calamity to give you a future and a hope" (Jeremiah 29:11).

God's plan includes that we become achievers in life. His desire is that we fulfill our responsibilities, accomplish the tasks he gives us, and overcome in the midst of life's inevitable struggles. He has not just given us a life assignment and then walked away or sat back to watch. He is continually available to help us as we ask him, listen to him, and follow his instructions.

The purpose of this book is to help you experience more successes in your life through learning and following twelve Keys to Success. These keys are applicable in our businesses and careers, in our relationships, and in our personal lives. You will learn about important attitudes and character traits that you can develop and important actions that you can take to more fully experience the blessings that God has for you. You will also learn how to avoid some common mistakes that could sabotage the plans and blessings God has for you.

We were created for success, but how shall we define success? To more readily address that question, let us consider three time frames: short-term, long-term, and eternal.

Short-term successes occur immediately or within a few days or weeks. Examples are passing a test in school, getting a date to the prom, doing our best in a sports activity, solving a problem or making a sale at work, or praying with someone and having him or her accept the Lord or be healed.

Long-term successes occur over a time span of months or years. Examples are graduating from high school; graduating from college; establishing a career, a business, or a ministry; developing a solid reputation; building a successful marriage; raising children; saving money and buying a home; or helping someone else build a successful life.

Eternal successes are the result of a lifetime of character development and accomplishments that adhere to God's principles. Our character and our accomplishments are both very important to God. It is commonly understood that we are not going to take any of our material possessions to heaven with us. However, we will take our record of deeds and accomplishments. We will know eternal success when we hear Jesus say, "Well done, my good and faithful servant. Enter into my joy.[1] Come live in my home.[2] Stay with me forever.[3]"

This book is based on many of God's instructions to us in the book of Proverbs. The material is organized around twelve Keys to Success:

1.   Establish a personal relationship with God.

2. Trust in God.
3. Walk humbly with God.
4. Deal honestly and truthfully with others.
5. Maintain your integrity.
6. Heed wise counsel.
7. Be diligent.
8. Treat everyone with respect.
9. Handle money wisely.
10. Beware of the love of money.
11. Avoid personal pitfalls.
12. Pray continually.

Even though it is God's desire and his plan that we be successful, successes will not come to us automatically. We will experience them as we adhere to God's instructions to us. I encourage you to apply these twelve Keys to Success. See for yourself that they are true!

1

ESTABLISH A PERSONAL RELATIONSHIP WITH GOD

One day a lawyer asked Jesus, "Teacher, which is the great commandment in the Law?" (Matthew 22:36).

Let me elaborate on what I believe was really in this lawyer's mind when he asked this question:

> "Teacher, there are many laws, rules, regulations, and commandments, including the Ten Commandments in the scriptures. In my training as a lawyer, I have carefully studied all of them. If I were to ask you to arrange them in the order of their importance to God, which would be number one? Which law is the most important to God?"

Without hesitating, Jesus replied by quoting Deuteronomy 6:5:

> And He said to him, "You shall love the Lord your God with all your heart, and with all your soul, and with all your mind. This is the great and foremost commandment" (Matthew 22:37–38).

Jesus' answer was that the most important thing we can do is have a love relationship with God. God is the source of all true blessings. Therefore, the beginning point for experiencing blessings and successes *from* God is to establish a personal relationship *with* God. The first Key to Success that we will study is: **Establish a personal relationship with God**.

Let's look more closely at Jesus' reply to the lawyer and see what we can learn about this relationship. We will focus our attention on *the Lord*, *your God*, and *love*.

THE LORD

Jesus said, "You shall love *the Lord...*" The words "the Lord" in Jesus' reply speak much about God. They tell us that God is the Lord: he is the ruler over everything. As the Lord, he has power and authority over every situation that we are facing or will ever face. Indeed, his power and authority far exceed anything that we can even imagine. There is no one anywhere who possesses or will ever possess greater power or authority than God has. It is very reassuring to know that he can utilize his power and authority on our behalf in any situation that we may face.

God is the Lord whether or not we know it. He is the Lord whether or not we ever admit it. He is the Lord regardless of how we feel about it. It is true because of who he is. *He is the Lord.*

YOUR GOD

Jesus said, "You shall love the Lord *your God...*" Let's next consider the phrase *your God*. These words address another type of relationship with him. You see, the Lord is not automatically *our* God. It is his plan and purpose that he be our God. He is ready and willing to be our God. He has taken every step except two to make that happen. It is up to us to take those last two steps. The first step is to *decide* that we want him to be our God. The second step is to *invite him* to become our God.

For many people, *deciding* to make the Lord their God is a very difficult step to take. It certainly was for me. This decision can be a hard one because we must first reach a point where we are willing to submit to him as our God, as the One whose authority we will acknowledge and obey in our lives. That decision involves a willingness to surrender many of our rights we want to keep for ourselves. It involves making a choice to follow his plans and purposes even when they may conflict with our own. Many people never become willing to make that decision. They live their entire lives without establishing a personal relationship with the Lord of the universe, in which he is available to guide, direct, bless, and protect them.

I cannot remember a time in my life that I did not believe that God exists, but I certainly did not always make him *my* God. The book of Hebrews pinpointed my situation when it said, " He who comes to God must believe that He is and that He is a rewarder of those who seek Him" (Hebrews 11:6b).

I was fortunate to have been brought up attending Sunday school and church. I never had to overcome agnostic or atheistic beliefs. It was always obvious to me that *God is*. But for the early part of my life, I did not know that he is a rewarder of those who seek him. I was very ignorant about God and his ways. I knew little of what he says about himself in the Bible because I had not read or studied the Bible. My knowledge of God was limited to what I learned from attending Sunday school and church. As a teenager and later as a young adult, I would have been willing to debate the issue of God as a rewarder, taking either side of the argument. But I would have been debating from the basis of "it seems to me that…" I could not have debated based on my biblical knowledge, my personal experiences, or even the experiences of friends or acquaintances.

The first time I was really challenged by someone to "accept Jesus" was when I was about fifteen. A youth evangelist came to one of the churches in my hometown, and nearly everyone in my high school attended at least one of the services. Many "went forward" to accept Jesus. I have a very logical mind, a very mathematical mind. My decisions are nearly always carefully weighed and thought out. I make very few impulsive or emotional decisions. When I was challenged to accept Jesus at this revival—to surrender my life to God—my thinking proceeded as follows: I mentally listed the advantages of surrendering my life to God. There was only one item on that list: to relieve any guilt that I might have about not surrendering to him. Since my guilt level was fairly low, this was not a pressing concern to me. The main item on my list of disadvantages was that surrendering to God would limit what I could do—the fun I thought I might have in high school and college and as a young adult. I understood that whenever we make a choice *for* something, it is also a choice *against* something else. Every choice we make restricts our remaining options. Since the disadvantages seemed to me to outweigh the advantages, I decided to postpone surrendering to God. I always intended to surrender to him someday, but only after I had enjoyed enough fun things in life, whatever they might turn out to be.

At subsequent challenges to surrender my life to God, I repeated this same line of reasoning and reached the same conclusion: the disadvantages outweighed the advantages.

I remember vividly where I was when my thinking changed. It was the fall of 1967, and I had recently begun work at Georgia Tech on a doctorate in electrical engineering. I was driving home to my apartment when the following thoughts that I knew were from God came into my mind:

> You are very intelligent and have been able to achieve
> much.

These words were factually true. By the age of twenty-four, I had earned a bachelor of science in electrical engineering, graduating summa cum laude and at the top of my engineering class at Louisiana Tech University. I had been married for two years to Brenda, a wonderful, beautiful, intelligent woman. During that time I had earned a master of science in electrical engineering at the University of Southern California. I had recently been awarded a fully paid fellowship to pursue my Ph.D. in electrical engineering at Georgia Tech.

The thoughts continued:

> If you have been able to do this well with your life by
> yourself, how much better could your life be if it were
> led by the Son of God?

I knew that Jesus was much wiser, more intelligent, more knowledgeable, and more experienced than I was. God's question made perfect sense to me. There was no possible answer other than, "My life would undoubtedly be much better if Jesus led it."

Not being impulsive and realizing that this would mean surrendering myself to God—something I had been previously unwilling to do—I began carefully considering this offer. I weighed the advantages against the disadvantages for two or three weeks. I concluded that it was very much to my advantage to accept God's offer to let Jesus lead my life. At that moment, without ever having read that scripture in the book of Hebrews, I somehow knew that "he is a rewarder of those who seek him." In all, it took me twenty-four years to complete the first step—*deciding* to invite the Lord into my life as my God.

After *deciding* to make the Lord our God, the other step we must take to initiate this relationship is to *invite him* to become our God. This only needs to take a few minutes, but those few minutes will change our lives forever. They certainly changed mine. You see, the moment we ask him to become our God, he accepts our invitation. He immediately gives us new life, a life that is alive to him. Jesus described it in John 3 as being *born again*, born of the Holy Spirit. Why does God give us this new life? He does it because *he loves us*, and he wants us to be members of his family. Furthermore, he wants his entire family to be continually with him, starting in this life and continuing throughout all eternity.

You may be thinking, "I'm not good enough, and I don't know if I could ever become good enough to deserve that kind of relationship with God." If that fact is what you are thinking, you are absolutely right. But this is no obstacle to God. He knows that none of us can ever be "good enough." In fact, no one except Jesus has ever been or could ever be "good enough."

The Apostle Paul, quoting from Psalm 14, wrote, "There is none righteous, not even one" (Romans 3:10). Later in the same chapter Paul wrote, "For all have sinned and fall short of the glory of God" (Romans 3:23).

Knowing that this would be the case with every one of us, God developed and implemented a plan whereby he could still become our God. Jesus, God's Son, lived a sinless life. While he was on the cross, God placed upon him all of the sins of the entire world. God placed on Jesus every sin that had ever been committed by anyone in the past, along with every sin that would ever be committed by anyone in the future. Then Jesus died and by his death paid the penalty for all of those sins. I don't fully understand how all this happened, but because of what the Bible says, I believe that it did happen. God foretold his plan of forgiveness hundreds of years earlier through the prophet Isaiah:

> All of us like sheep have gone astray,
> Each of us has turned to his own way;
> But the Lord has caused the iniquity of us all
> To fall on Him (Isaiah 53:6).

In early November of 1967, I asked the Rev. Claude Smithmier, the pastor of the Methodist church that my wife and I had begun attending, to visit us in our apartment. Sitting at the kitchen table with him and my wife (who without my knowledge had been praying for my salvation for the previous four years), I told him that I had never accepted Jesus as my personal savior, and I was now ready to do so. He led me in a simple prayer of confession, repentance, and acceptance. That day I surrendered my life to God and asked Jesus to become my Savior and my Lord. And Jesus did. I have never for a moment regretted making that decision and praying that prayer. I have often regretted not having done it earlier in my life.

LOVE

Jesus said, "You shall *love* the Lord your God with all your heart, and with all your soul, and with all your mind" (Matthew 22:37, italics added).

The significance of the word *love* is that God desires our relationship with him to be one of mutual love. Not fear, not duty, but mutual love. In this, the Great Commandment, God is not requiring us to do more than he is doing. If he were requiring that we love him more than he loves us, he would be unfair. In that case, he would be demanding unrequited love from us. It is impossible for him to be unfair. We therefore know from this scripture verse that he loves us with his whole being.

How can we describe God's love for us? Jesus said, "For God so loved the world, that He gave His only begotten Son, that whoever believes in Him shall not perish, but have eternal life" (John 3:16). The Apostle Paul wrote:

> For while we were still helpless, at the right time Christ died for the ungodly. For one will hardly die for a righteous man; though perhaps for the good man someone would dare even to die. But God demonstrates His own love toward us, in that while we were yet sinners, Christ died for us (Romans 5:6–8).

1 Corinthians 13 is often called the Love Chapter of the Bible. It is frequently read at weddings. It is often preached about as the ideal for how we are to love one another. That is certainly a valid application of the chapter. But 1 Corinthians 13 also very much describes God's love for us. To make that point easier to see, let's look at a few verses and substitute "God's love for us" wherever the verse says "love."

> [God's love for us] is patient, [God's love for us] is kind and is not jealous; [God's love for us] does not brag and is not arrogant, does not act unbecomingly; it does not seek its own, is not provoked, does not take into account a wrong suffered, does not rejoice in unrighteousness, but rejoices with the truth; bears all things, believes all things, hopes all things, endures all things. [God's love for us] never fails (1 Corinthians 13:4–8a).

These verses let us know unequivocally that God loves us. Matthew 22:37 says that he wants us to love him. In fact, he wants the relationship between us and him to grow and develop until we so fully realize and experience his love for us that we freely love him with *all* our heart, and with *all* our soul, and with *all* our mind (Matthew 22:37). That kind of love cannot be achieved quickly. It takes time to develop and grow.

Love in any relationship has a beginning point. It develops from that beginning point as it is nurtured and nourished. Our love for God begins when we first recognize that he loves us and we begin responding to his love. The love between him and us grows as we jointly nurture our relationship. As this love relationship grows, we realize and experience more and more how much God truly loves us. Our natural response to his love is to love him even more. And so this relationship of love never stops growing, for we can never exhaust the riches of the love of God.

PLAN OF ACTION

How do you establish a personal relationship with God? There are two simple steps. The first step is to *decide* to make him your God. If you have already made this decision, then you are ready for the second step. If you have not yet made this decision but are ready, simply tell him, "Lord, I want you to be my God." That is all you need to do to complete the first step of making him your God.

Suppose you are not yet ready to make him your God, but you are *willing to become ready*. Then confirm that to him by saying, "Lord, please help me become willing to ask you to be my God." I promise that he will work with you and help you get ready to make that decision.

The second step is to *invite* God to become your God. You can do this by praying a prayer such as the following one:

> God, I believe that Jesus is your Son. I choose to believe the Bible when it says that he died for my sins, was buried, and was raised from the dead on the third day.[1] I ask you to become my God. I relinquish my old life to you, and I accept the new life that you now give me. Thank you for hearing and answering my prayer. Amen.

If you pray this prayer or one like it, God will indeed give you a new life, a life from himself. It begins as soon as you pray. You establish a personal relationship with him. He becomes *your God*. This relationship is a permanent one. No one can ever take it away from you, for God will not let him.

Once you have established your personal relationship with God, you need to begin learning about him and experiencing his love. In fact, your relationship should grow and develop throughout the rest of your life. A good idea is to find someone such as a pastor or a Christian friend who will be able to help and encourage you to grow in your relationship of love with the Lord your God.

2

TRUST IN GOD

The second Key to Success is: **Trust in God**. What does that mean? To trust in God is to continually rely on him for whatever we need and to have confidence that he will not fail us. This chapter is about how to begin trusting God. This Key, along with most of the Keys to Success that we are studying, is based primarily on scriptures from the book of Proverbs. It is important to note that Solomon, who wrote most of the book of Proverbs, says:

> So that your trust may be in the Lord,
> I have taught you today, even you.
> Have I not written to you excellent things
> Of counsels and knowledge,
> To make you know the certainty of the words of truth
> That you may correctly answer to him who sent you?
>   (Proverbs 22:19–22).

One of the declared purposes of the book of Proverbs is to help us learn to trust in the Lord, so we can be certain that trusting in God is important to our success.

Proverbs 3:5 is a well-known verse that counsels us to trust in God:

> Trust in the Lord with all your heart
> And do not lean on your own understanding.

Another verse is Psalm 37:3a:

> Trust in the Lord and do good.

One more is Psalm 62:8a:

> Trust in Him at all times, O people.

We see from these verses that the Bible says we *should* trust in the Lord. Why should we trust him? What benefits are there? Are we being told to trust in him simply because it is the proper thing to do, or are there more compelling reasons? Most assuredly there are more compelling reasons, and here are a few of them. Do we want to be blessed in our health, relationships, emotional well-being, and in our relationship with God? Then we must learn to trust the Lord.

> He who gives attention to the word will find good,
> And blessed is he who trusts in the Lord
> > (Proverbs 16:20).

Do we want to prosper in our careers and our finances? Then we must learn to trust the Lord.

> An arrogant man stirs up strife,
> But he who trusts in the Lord will prosper
> > (Proverbs 28:25).

Do we want advancement in our careers, our reputation among our colleagues, and our standing in the community? Then we must learn to trust the Lord.

> The fear of man brings a snare,
> But he who trusts in the Lord will be exalted
> > (Proverbs 29:25).

In these and in many other verses the Bible declares that it will be very beneficial to us if we will trust in the Lord.

At the time I made the decision to surrender my life and my future to God, my level of confidence in him was not very high. I did not yet look to him for guidance, protection, or provision. That was natural since our relationship was just starting. I had no personal history to draw upon in which I had trusted him in specific instances and had seen his faithfulness to me as events unfolded. Furthermore, at that point I did not know how to believe and act upon what he said in the Bible.

A natural question to ask is, "How can we learn to trust in God?" Fortunately, learning to trust in him is not difficult or complex. It is based on understanding and believing five fundamental facts about him:

1. He is trustworthy.
2. He created us and knows us personally.
3. He loves us.
4. He knows the things we need.
5. He will provide for us as we seek him.

Let us look at some scriptures that declare to us that each of these facts is true, and we can rely on them. When we acknowledge these facts about God, we will have a basis for putting our trust in him.

HE IS TRUSTWORTHY

To say that God is trustworthy is to declare that he is reliable, he is dependable, and he is worthy of our trust. Time after time throughout history, God has shown himself to be trustworthy. Scripture after scripture in the Bible declares that he is trustworthy. Here are four such scriptures:

> Every word of God is tested;
> He is a shield to those who take refuge in Him
>   (Proverbs 30:5).
>
> As for God, His way is blameless;
> The word of the Lord is tried;
> He is a shield to all who take refuge in Him
>   (Psalm 18:30).
>
> In You our fathers trusted;
> They trusted and You delivered them.
> To You they cried out and were delivered;
> In You they trusted and were not disappointed
>   (Psalm 22:4–5).
>
> Trust in the Lord forever,
> For in God the Lord, we have an everlasting Rock
>   (Isaiah 26:4).

These scriptures assure us that *God is trustworthy*.

HE CREATED US AND KNOWS US PERSONALLY

That God created us and knows us is presented explicitly and beautifully in Psalm 139. Psalm 139 is not only speaking about God's relationship to David, who wrote the psalm; it is also speaking about God's relationship to *us*. Verses 13 to 16 tell how he lovingly created each of us.

> For You formed my inward parts;
> You wove me in my mother's womb.
> I will give thanks to You, for I am fearfully and
>   wonderfully made;
> Wonderful are Your works,
> And my soul knows it very well.
> My frame was not hidden from You,

> When I was made in secret,
> And skillfully wrought in the depths of the earth;
> Your eyes have seen my unformed substance;
> And in Your book were all written
> The days that were ordained for me,
> When as yet there was not one of them
>   (Psalm 139:13–16).

These verses let us know that none of us are accidents in God's eyes. Regardless of how much our parents wanted us, he wanted us. He planned us, he created us, and he gave us life. These verses also declare that he has a plan for each person's life, a customized plan that he himself developed.

Verses 1 to 4 of this psalm beautifully affirm that he knows us intimately and continually watches over us.

> O Lord, You have searched me and known me.
> You know when I sit down and when I rise up;
> You understand my thought from afar.
> You scrutinize my path and my lying down,
> And are intimately acquainted with all my ways.
> Even before there is a word on my tongue,
> Behold, O Lord, You know it all
>   (Psalm 139:1–4).

God knows us. He knows everything that we are and everything that we have ever done. He knows much more about us, our ways, and our thoughts than we know about ourselves. *God created us and knows us personally.*

HE LOVES US

Another fact upon which we can build our trust in God is that *he loves us.* Regardless of the events going on around us, regardless of how our circumstances may look, and regardless of how we feel at the moment, God loves us unfailingly. I especially like the way the Apostle Paul expressed it in his letter to the Romans.

Before we look at what Paul wrote about God's love, let me tell you a little about Paul. He had been personally visited by Jesus a number of years after the resurrection. Later Paul had been transported by God to heaven to see its glory. He had also suffered persecutions, beatings, imprisonments, death threats, shipwrecks, and stoning. After having experienced all of these things, he wrote the following to help us understand the power of God's love for us:

> Who will separate us from the love of Christ? Will tribulation, or distress, or persecution, or famine, or nakedness, or peril, or sword? Just as it is written,
>> "For Your sake we are being put to death all day long;
>> We were considered as sheep to be slaughtered."
> But in all these things we overwhelmingly conquer through Him who loved us. For I am convinced that neither death, nor life, nor angels, nor principalities, nor things present, nor things to come, nor powers, nor height, nor depth, nor any other created thing, will be able to separate us from the love of God, which is in Christ Jesus our Lord (Romans 8:35–39).

This scripture assures us that *God loves us,* and there is nothing anywhere that has enough power to deflect that love.

HE KNOWS THE THINGS WE NEED

One of the most well-known and beloved portions of the Bible is Jesus' Sermon on the Mount. In this sermon Jesus reminds his followers that God provides for the material needs of all the animals, even ones as insignificant and unimpressive to us as sparrows. He cares for the plants—those as beautiful as lilies and those as ordinary as grass. Because Jesus says that God cares for all these other things in his creation, which are of much less importance to him than we are, we can be absolutely certain that he cares for us. Jesus continues his sermon by encouraging his followers:

> Do not worry then, saying, "What will we eat?" or "What will we drink?" or "What will we wear for clothing?" For the Gentiles eagerly seek all these things; for your heavenly Father knows that you need all these things (Matthew 6:31–32).

God knows that we need food to eat, water to drink, and clothes to wear. He knows that we need a place to live, a job, people to love, people to love us, and a purpose for our lives. Jesus assures us that *God knows the things we need.*

HE WILL PROVIDE FOR US AS WE SEEK HIM

In the next verse, Jesus tells us:

> But seek first His kingdom and His righteousness, and all these things will be added to you (Matthew 6:33).

Jesus sets forth a priority: seek *first* his kingdom. We are to put God first, ahead of our careers, our finances, our leisure activities, our hopes, and our dreams. And what will happen when we put *him* first? He will put *us* first in *his* priorities, and he will provide us with the things we need: food, water, clothes, a place to live, a job, people to love, people to love us, and a purpose in life. But he won't stop there. He will also provide us with peace, joy, and fulfillment beyond anything we could even imagine.

At this point you might be thinking, "I need some of those things. When can I expect to get them? How can I be sure that I will have them when I need them?" Jesus said that we will get these things as we seek God's kingdom and his righteousness in our lives. He continued his sermon by telling us not to worry or be anxious about when we will get such provisions.

> So do not worry about tomorrow; for tomorrow will care for itself. Each day has enough trouble of its own (Matthew 6:34).

When we become anxious about something, it often is an indication that our trust in God needs strengthening. We must resist letting ourselves worry or become anxious. Instead we must choose to trust in God, for Jesus has said that *God will provide for us as we seek him.*

To summarize, there are five important reasons why we can and should trust God:

1. He is trustworthy.
2. He created us and knows us personally.
3. He loves us.
4. He knows the things we need.
5. He will provide for us as we seek him.

Trusting in God is active, not passive. It requires our focus and conscious commitment. For instance, it requires that we choose to trust *God* for our future, and that we turn from trusting in other things or ideas.

ALTERNATIVES TO TRUSTING IN GOD

One alternative to trusting in God is to live in fear. Trust in God helps us overcome fear.

> When I am afraid,
> I will put my trust in You.
> In God, whose word I praise,
> In God I have put my trust;
> I shall not be afraid.
> What can mere man do to me?
>   (Psalm 56:3–4).

> Behold, God is my salvation,
> I will trust and not be afraid;
> For the Lord God is my strength and song,
> And He has become my salvation (Isaiah 12:2).

The book of Proverbs warns against two other specific things that people often trust in. The first is riches.

> He who trusts in his riches will fall,
> But the righteous will flourish like the green leaf
>   (Proverbs 11:28).

Riches are not trustworthy. The Bible says that if we trust in riches, there will come a time when we need them and they will not be there for us. But God is trustworthy. He is always there for us.

The second thing the Bible warns us against is trusting in ourselves, especially trusting our own assessment of a situation.

> Trust in the Lord with all your heart
> And do not lean on your own understanding.
> In all your ways acknowledge Him,
> And He will make your paths straight
>   (Proverbs 3:5–6).

These verses confirm that none of us are fully trustworthy with our own future. One reason is that we cannot know with any certainty what our future will be like—what events and circumstances we will have to face and what choices will confront us. Even if we did know those things, we would not always have sufficient wisdom or knowledge to handle whatever comes our way. But God does know the future. He knows what will be coming our way, and he has all the wisdom and knowledge needed to help us handle whatever may happen. If we are to succeed, we must be careful not to trust in riches and not to trust only in our own understanding. We must learn to *trust in God.*

Our trusting in God starts with a personal decision to begin trusting him. It then continues throughout the remainder of our lives as we consciously trust him daily. Jesus taught us in the Lord's Prayer to trust God daily: "Give us this day our daily bread" (Matthew 6:11).

Some days it is easy to trust him. Other days it can be very hard, especially when we do not understand or agree with our circumstances at that moment.

Bob and Ellen (not their real names) are long-time friends of me and my wife. Many years ago they decided to trust God with their future, and they have lived out that decision daily to the best of their ability.

During the Easter holidays of 1998, they were visiting in Wisconsin with their daughter, son-in-law, and grandson. After Easter Bob flew home, but Ellen decided to stay a little longer. A few days later, she was in the house alone when she became immobilized by excruciating pains in her head. She cried out, "God, send help!" and then put her trust in him. Within a short time, her daughter returned home, saw the situation and called 911. Ellen was whisked to a local hospital where a CAT scan revealed extensive bleeding inside her skull.

A medical helicopter was summoned and flew her to a Mayo Health System facility, where a top neurosurgeon was on call. By the time she arrived, her left side was almost completely paralyzed. The neurosurgeon later said he was amazed that she was still alive.

A cerebral angiogram and another CAT scan resulted in a diagnosis of "right temporal lobe intracerebral hematoma, from probable rupture of arteriovenous malformation." In layman's terms, malformed blood vessels in her head had ruptured and flooded her brain with blood. This blood had then coagulated into a massive clot.

The neurosurgeon asked the hospital chaplain to have Ellen's daughter and son-in-law come into the operating room and say goodbye because he was certain that she would not survive the upcoming surgery. If she did live, she would likely be completely incapacitated due to severe neurological damage.

After speaking to her mother, Ellen's daughter, son-in-law, and one of their Christian friends began praying earnestly. When Ellen heard them praying, an indescribable feeling of peace engulfed her as she lay on the operating table. She thought, "This is wonderful. I am going home to be with Jesus!" Then she heard the most joyous laughter and a voice that said, "No, God is not through with you there. There are still many people who need your encouragement." As Ellen pondered these words, the surgeons put her under anesthesia and began the dangerous procedure.

During surgery, the neurosurgeon removed the damaged right temporal lobe of Ellen's brain, along with the clot and the malformed blood vessels. To the astonishment of the medical team, Ellen awoke from the surgery with her full mental faculties and no evidence of any paralysis! The hospital staff began referring to her as "the woman who should be dead." She was released from the hospital after only four days and became a living testimony to the trustworthiness of the God in whom she trusted.

THE BLESSINGS OF TRUSTING IN GOD

We began this chapter by looking at three scriptures that promise blessing, prosperity, and promotion for those who trust in the Lord. I close the chapter with two scriptures that include some of the many other blessings that will come to us as we trust in the Lord.

David states in the Psalms that God will give us the desires of our hearts as we trust and delight in him:

> Trust in the Lord and do good;
> Dwell in the land and cultivate faithfulness.
> Delight yourself in the Lord;
> And He will give you the desires of your heart.
> Commit your way to the Lord,
> Trust also in Him, and He will do it (Psalm 37:3–5).

And the prophet Jeremiah declares that we will be sustained by God and continue to be fruitful, even in difficult times, as we trust in him:

> Blessed is the man who trusts in the Lord
> And whose trust is the Lord.
> For he will be like a tree planted by the water,
> That extends its roots by a stream

> And will not fear when the heat comes;
> But its leaves will be green,
> And it will not be anxious in a year of drought
> Nor cease to yield fruit (Jeremiah 17:7–8).

We will begin to experience the blessings of God as we learn to trust in him. *Trust in God.*

PLAN OF ACTION

Trusting in God begins with a decision to trust him and continues as we consciously trust him daily. Start by reviewing the scriptures in this chapter. Decide to believe them and to trust in God daily. Declare with David:

> But as for me, I trust in You , O Lord,
> I say, "You are my God" (Psalm 31:14).

After making this decision, refuse to turn back. Continually re-affirm your decision to trust in God. We build our trust in God as we consciously act on the scriptures in this chapter and look for the blessings that God has promised to all who trust in him.

3

WALK HUMBLY WITH GOD

T he prophet Micah, speaking about God, says:

> He has told you, O man, what is good;
> And what does the Lord require of you
> But to do justice, to love kindness,
> And to walk humbly with your God? (Micah 6:8).

The third Key to Success is: **Walk humbly with God**.

Some people get a very negative impression when a person is described as being humble. They get a perception of weakness—of someone with a poor self-image who lacks self-confidence, ambition, and initiative. This is not at all what this verse means. It means to not be arrogant, proud, or pretentious, but instead to be teachable and respectful of who God is.

Walk

The phrase "walk humbly with God" is not passive; it is active. The verb "walk" denotes motion and movement. It speaks of going somewhere. This scripture does not tell us to lie down, kneel, sit, or stand. Those postures each have their place in our relationship with God, but this Key to Success addresses walking.

WALK WITH GOD

Now let's expand our view to encompass the words "walk...with God." Envision God going somewhere and us accompanying him. Many times we instead start going somewhere and ask God to accompany us. Even though he will often graciously do so, it is best if we let him lead, choose the path and set the pace.

There is another important aspect of our walk with God. It should not be a case of us tagging along behind him. The emphasis of the word "with" suggests being at his side wherever the journey may lead. We must be sure we do not get ahead of him or lag behind, but travel side by side with him.

Notice that the verse does not mention a destination. It does not say something like "walk with God until you reach such and such a place or condition." The point of the verse is not for us to reach a particular destination. The point is for us to be together with him on a journey and to enjoy close communion and fellowship with him as we travel. It is to receive the knowledge and wisdom that he imparts to us as we journey with him. It is to rejoice as we realize that God is going to continually accomplish something significant, and we are going to be a participant in it with him.

HUMBLY

Once we get a picture of "walking with God" planted in our minds, the attitude part—humbly—falls more easily into place. As long as we are walking with God, following his lead, moving toward his goals, and are aware of how much his wisdom, power, and abilities exceed our own, there is little room for pride to arise within us. There is little room for pretense or arrogance because he is leading and we are merely accompanying him.

PRIDE

Walking humbly with God is the preventative for the dangers that pride brings. The word *pride* has both positive and negative meanings. Pride in a positive sense is dignity and self-respect. It is satisfaction in our work and enjoyment of our achievements. Positive pride delights in the blessings that God has bestowed on us.

Pride in the negative sense manifests itself as conceit, arrogance, and self-satisfaction. God warns us repeatedly throughout the book of Proverbs to beware of this kind of pride. One reason God warns us against negative pride is because it leads us to depend upon ourselves rather than to seek his guidance and counsel in dealing with situations we face. It leads us to depend upon our own abilities instead of depending upon his abilities. Under the influence of pride, we set our own goals and then chart our own course to achieve those goals instead of walking humbly with him. Pride can easily lead us astray from God's plan for our lives and will by its very nature make it difficult for us to recognize our error and turn back to him.

Let's look at some scriptures in the book of Proverbs that warn us against pride.

> Pride goes before destruction,
> And a haughty spirit before stumbling
>   (Proverbs 16:18).

We often hear this scripture paraphrased as, "Pride goes before a fall." Why does such a thing happen to so many people? One reason is that when we are being led by our pride, we become overconfident of our abilities, and we cease to be properly vigilant. Two scriptures speak about this.

> Do not be wise in your own eyes;
> Fear the Lord and turn away from evil (Proverbs 3:7).

> A wise man is cautious and turns away from evil,
> But a fool is arrogant and careless (Proverbs 14:16).

Another reason that pride goes before a fall is that we can easily become overconfident about our own plans and ignore God's plans. Several scriptures speak to this.

> Do not boast about tomorrow,
> For you do not know what a day may bring forth
>   (Proverbs 27:1).

James amplified on this point in his letter to the early church.

> Come now, you who say, "Today or tomorrow we will go to such and such a city, and spend a year there and engage in business and make a profit." Yet you do not know what your life will be like tomorrow. You are just a vapor that appears for a little while and then vanishes away. Instead, you ought to say, "If the Lord wills, we will live and also do this or that." But as it is, you boast in your arrogance; all such boasting is evil (James 4:13–16).

Notice that James provided an antidote to pride when he wrote:

> Instead, you ought to say, "If the Lord wills, we will live and also do this or that" (James 4:15).

We should always leave room in our plans for the possibility that God may have different plans, plans that we currently do not know about. *Walk humbly with God*, and be teachable and flexible.

HONOR

There is an unexpected result that the Bible says follows from humility: *honor*. To receive honor is to receive recognition, admiration, and respect. A very important aspect of honor is that we cannot achieve it directly. Honor is bestowed by others when they recognize something admirable in a person. The book of Proverbs says:

> Let another praise you, and not your own mouth;
> A stranger, and not your own lips (Proverbs 27:2).

Notice how the following scriptures link humility and honor.

> When pride comes, then comes dishonor,
> But with the humble is wisdom (Proverbs 11:2).

> The fear of the Lord is the instruction for wisdom,
> And before honor comes humility (Proverbs 15:33).

> Before destruction the heart of man is haughty,
> But humility goes before honor (Proverbs 18:12).

> A man's pride will bring him low,
> But a humble spirit will obtain honor
>   (Proverbs 29:23).

Pride and arrogance are like masks. They hide the aspects of our character and accomplishments that would bring us true honor, recognition, admiration, and respect. Humility, on the other hand, is like a transparent window. Through humility, a person's true character and accomplishments can be clearly seen by others.

There is probably no more striking example of a person of humility being bestowed with honor upon honor than that of Mother Teresa. At an early age this plain, humble woman unreservedly accepted God's call to go as a missionary to India. In 1946 she accepted God's call within a call, as she referred to it. She was to live among and freely serve the poorest of the poor, showing them God's love.

She began bringing in dying, destitute people from the streets of Calcutta, a few at a time, to ease their suffering with love, kindness, a cheerful atmosphere, and a place to die in peace. Others joined with her to help in the work.

As time progressed, she opened houses for lepers, for orphans, for the mentally ill, for the outcasts of society. She—and those with her—ministered to each person individually as if that person were Jesus himself disguised as the needy person. Workers continually joined with her. The work grew and expanded, first within India and then to other countries around the world. But the work never lost its original focus of freely serving the poorest of the poor.

I suppose Mother Teresa was bestowed with more honors during her lifetime than any other person of her era. In 1973 she was given the very first Templeton Prize for Progress in Religion. At a million dollars, it was the world's largest monetary prize. She was awarded honorary doctorate degrees from St. Francis Xavier University in Nova Scotia in 1975, Viswa Bharati University in India in 1976, and the University of Cambridge in 1977. In 1979 she was awarded the Nobel Peace Prize. Honors continued to be bestowed upon her by governments, universities, and organizations throughout the world until her death in 1997. She graciously accepted each award because she said it gave her an opportunity to speak about Christ to people who might otherwise not hear about him, and to make people aware of the poor. The money she received went to continue her work of helping the poor.

Throughout her life she remained committed to a life of simplicity, humility, and service to the poorest of the poor throughout the world. Yet she was also a friend and guest of the Pope and of kings, presidents, and heads of government too numerous to name. At the time of her death, the work that she had started was being carried on by thousands of sisters, brothers, and co-workers in more than a hundred countries.[1]

HUMILITY AS A PRIORITY

The Lord values our humility more highly than our monetary success, for the Bible says:

> It is better to be humble in spirit with the lowly
> Than to divide the spoil with the proud (Proverbs
>   16:19).

When we "divide the spoil," we are acquiring wealth as a reward for a conquest. God says in this verse that he would rather we be humble than rich. *Therefore, if we want to achieve monetary success through God's favor, it is imperative that we align our priorities with his on the issue of humility.*

I close this chapter with a wonderful promise from God that links humility, honor, riches, and life. The riches promised are not limited to financial riches. They include whatever we need, in the measure of abundance that only God can supply.

The reward of humility and the fear of the Lord
Are riches, honor and life (Proverbs 22:4).

Plan of Action

I knew a pastor who often jokingly said that some day he was going to preach a sermon titled "The Seven Steps to Humility, and How I Achieved It." The implication is that if we think that we are humble, then obviously we are not. Humility does not come from our conscious efforts to achieve it. *Humility comes as we understand the insignificance of our own abilities compared to the greatness of God's abilities.* Humility comes as we understand that, in spite of who we are and what we may have done in the past, God still loves us and wants us to walk beside him. Humility comes as we get to know him in all his glory, splendor, and majesty.

Let us make the decision to walk humbly with God, wherever he leads. As we start out, our emphasis should just be on "walking with God." Seek to learn what he is doing and how he wants us to participate; then join him wholeheartedly in it. Humility will grow in us as we walk with him.

4

DEAL HONESTLY AND TRUTHFULLY WITH OTHERS

God always deals honestly and truthfully with us, and he wants us to deal that way with others. This chapter addresses the fourth Key to Success: **Deal honestly and truthfully with others**.

HONESTY

To deal honestly and truthfully is to conduct business ethically, openly, and with integrity. It is to deal without lying, cheating, or deceit.

When I was growing up in a small town in the South, a person's reputation was very important. Because it was a small town and people knew one another, it was normal to "ask around town" to find out about a person's reputation before deciding whether or not to do business with him. Similarly, before deciding to hire someone, a prospective employer would inquire about that person from people who knew him and from people who had previously employed him. *A person's honesty was a major factor in establishing his or her reputation!*

What is God's attitude toward honesty? The following verses demonstrate that conducting our business honestly is very important to God:

> A false balance is an abomination to the Lord,
> But a just weight is His delight (Proverbs 11:1).

A just balance and scales belong to the Lord;
All the weights of the bag are His concern
    (Proverbs 16:11).

Differing weights and differing measures,
Both of them are abominable to the Lord
    (Proverbs 20:10).

Differing weights are an abomination to the Lord,
And a false scale is not good (Proverbs 20:23).

These verses directly address honesty in conducting business. Notice that they each contain essentially the same message. Because this message is presented not just once or twice, but four times, we can be certain that it is very important. Also notice that the Bible phrases the message slightly differently in each verse. This is to help us better grasp the message and to give us a more robust explanation of what God is saying. He wants us to know that he *delights* in honesty, and that dishonesty is an *abomination* to him. An abomination is something disgusting, loathsome, and repulsive. We need not expect God to bless and prosper us if we conduct our business in a way that is disgusting to him.

WEIGHTS, SCALES, AND MEASURES

What is the significance of the weights, scales, and measures that are mentioned in these scriptures? In biblical times, weights, scales, and measures were used in the marketplace to determine the weight or volume of the product being sold. Wheat, flour, meal, olive oil, wine, and meat were some of the everyday items that would need to be weighed or measured to determine their price. Because coins were not always of uniform weight, it was also normal practice to weigh them to determine their value before completing a sale. The process of weighing and measuring products and coins provided numerous opportunities for a dishonest person to cheat those he or she bought from or sold to.

When I buy a gallon of bulk olive oil, if I fill a container that I know is larger than a gallon, I am being dishonest. When I sell a bushel of wheat, if I measure it out using a container that I know is smaller than a bushel, I am being dishonest. When I sell a piece of meat, if I weigh it with weights that are lighter than they should be, I am being dishonest. When I weigh coins presented to me toward a purchase, if I use weights that are heavier than they should be, or if I use an improperly balanced scale, I am being dishonest.

A person who uses dishonest weights, scales, and measures has sold his or her honesty. He or she may make a larger profit on a given transaction, but that person has become a crook, a deceiver, and a cheat. If we choose to conduct our business that way, it is highly damaging to our relationship with God. It cuts us off from many of the blessings that he would like to bestow upon us.

What must we do? We must deal honestly and truthfully. To make this easier to do, we must get rid of all the schemes and devices which could tempt us to deal dishonestly. We must get rid of our "false weights, scales, and measures." Then the Lord can smile upon and bless our businesses and our careers. Regarding this matter, God declared clearly:

> You shall not have in your bag differing weights, a large and a small. You shall not have in your house differing measures, a large and a small. You shall have a full and just weight; you shall have a full and just measure, that your days may be prolonged in the land which the Lord your God gives you. For everyone who does these things, everyone who acts unjustly is

an abomination to the Lord your God (Deuteronomy
25:13–16).

We have modern government regulations, inspections,
and enforcement. One might think that cheating with
dishonest weights and measures would be fairly infrequent
today, especially in the United States. Is it really? Suppose
someone delivers thirty-eight loaves of bread to a grocery
store, charges for forty, and pockets the difference. Is this
not a dishonest measure? Suppose someone sends 9.5
cubic yards of concrete to a construction site, charges for
10 yards, and pockets the difference. Is this not a dishonest
measure? Suppose someone works thirty-eight hours one
week, reports working forty , and accepts a full paycheck. Is
that not a dishonest measure?

When we are dishonest, we harm other people. God
loves us, and it is important to him that we be honest. God
loves everyone else, too, and he wants us to *deal honestly
with each of them*. Let us *deal honestly and truthfully with
others* so that we may be more pleasing to God.

The Bible says that *it is better in God's eyes to be honest
than to be rich*.

> Better is the poor who walks in his integrity
> Than he who is crooked though he be rich
>   (Proverbs 28:6).

> For the devious are an abomination to the Lord;
> But He is intimate with the upright (Proverbs 3:32).

PLAN OF ACTION

Let us make the decision to deal honestly and truthfully
with others because it is pleasing to God. If we have been

less than honest in our dealings in the past, what should we do? The Apostle Paul provided the answer:

> He who steals must steal no longer; but rather he must labor, performing with his own hands what is good, so that he will have something to share with one who has need (Ephesians 4:28).

5

MAINTAIN YOUR INTEGRITY

We will address in this chapter the fifth Key to Success, which is: **Maintain your integrity**. *Integrity* is firm adherence to a strict code of ethics. It implies undeviating steadfastness in matters pertaining to principle, responsibility, honor, or trust. When I first began reading the book of Proverbs, searching for guidance on how to conduct business God's way, I came away with the impression that integrity was an important trait to have. However, my impression was simply that "integrity is a good thing," and therefore being a person of integrity is pleasing to God. I later discovered that I had completely missed the point. To discover why integrity is important, let's look at three verses.

> He who walks in integrity walks securely,
> But he who perverts his ways will be found out
> (Proverbs 10:9).

> The integrity of the upright will guide them,
> But the crookedness of the treacherous will destroy
> them (Proverbs 11:3).

> The righteousness of the upright will deliver them,
> But the treacherous will be caught by their own
> greed (Proverbs 11:6).

YOUR INTEGRITY PROTECTS YOU

You see, whereas the main purpose of our *honesty* is to protect other people, the main purpose of our *integrity* is to protect *us*. God loves us very much. He does not want our reputation to be damaged (Proverbs 10:9), nor does he want treachery to destroy us (Proverbs 11:3,6). In other words, we need integrity to prevent us from doing things that could harm or even destroy us.

God, speaking through the prophet Jeremiah, said:

> "For I know the plans that I have for you," declares the Lord, "plans for welfare and not for calamity to give you a future and a hope" (Jeremiah 29:11).

God wants what is good for us. He wants us to have success, a future, and a hope. Those verses in the book of Proverbs warn us that we need integrity to guard us against being sidetracked and derailed from God's purposes for us.

David understood that we live in a dangerous world. He also understood the role of integrity in protecting us in this world.

> Look upon my enemies, for they are many,
> And they hate me with violent hatred.
> Guard my soul and deliver me;
> Do not let me be ashamed, for I take refuge in You.
> Let integrity and uprightness preserve me,
> For I wait for You (Psalm 25:19–21).

In this psalm, David asked the Lord to guard him and deliver him from his enemies as he took refuge in the Lord. But he also asked the Lord to let integrity and upright-ness preserve him. In another psalm, David declared that the Lord himself would protect the upright person (or the person of integrity) against harm from evildoers.

> The wicked plots against the righteous
> And gnashes at him with his teeth.
> The Lord laughs at him,
> For He sees his day is coming.
> The wicked have drawn the sword and bent their bow
> To cast down the afflicted and the needy,
> To slay those who are upright in conduct.
> Their sword will enter their own heart,
> And their bows will be broken (Psalm 37:12–15).

AN EXAMPLE FROM SCRIPTURE

There is an enlightening incident in Genesis 20 involving Abraham, his wife Sarah, and a local king named Abimelech. In this incident God protected Abraham and Sarah from harm because of his covenant with them, but he also protected King Abimelech because he was a man of integrity.

A brief background of the story is that kings in those days had absolute authority in their kingdoms over life, death, and property. Sarah was a beautiful woman, and Abraham was afraid that some king would kill him so that he could take Sarah as one of his wives or concubines. As Abraham and Sarah journeyed from place to place, Abraham intro-duced Sarah as his sister, instead of saying that she was his wife. She was, in fact, his half-sister. Abraham said this so that if a king chose to take Sarah as his wife, the king would not first kill Abraham because he was Sarah's husband. (See Genesis 12:10–20 for an example.)

The incident with King Abimelech began this way:

> Now Abraham journeyed from there toward the land
> of the Negev, and settled between Kadesh and Shur;
> then he sojourned in Gerar. Abraham said of Sarah
> his wife, "She is my sister" So Abimelech king of Gerar
> sent and took Sarah. But God came to Abimelech in a
> dream of the night, and said to him, "Behold, you are
> a dead man because of the woman whom you have
> taken, for she is married" (Genesis 20:1–3).

I can't even begin to imagine how terrified I would be
if God himself came to me in a dream, pointed his finger
at me, and proclaimed, "You are a dead man!" because of
something I had just done. For one thing, I would be absolutely certain that I would not be going to the good place.
The story continued:

> Now Abimelech had not come near her; and he said,
> "Lord, will You slay a nation, even though blameless?
> Did he not himself say to me, 'She is my sister'? And
> she herself said, 'He is my brother' In the integrity of
> my heart and the innocence of my hands I have done
> this." Then God said to him in the dream, "Yes, I know
> that in the integrity of your heart you have done this,
> and I also kept you from sinning against Me; therefore
> I did not let you touch her. Now therefore, restore the
> man's wife, for he is a prophet, and he will pray for you
> and you will live. But if you do not restore her, know
> that you shall surely die, you and all who are yours"
> (Genesis 20:4–7).

The remainder of Genesis 20 recounts the subsequent
events: the conversation between Abimelech, Abraham,
and Sarah; that Abraham prayed to God for Abimelech; and
that God released Abimelech from the consequences of his

mistake. The point to notice is that Abimelech's integrity saved him when he had made a potentially deadly mistake.

OUR CODE OF ETHICS

We defined integrity as firm adherence to a strict code of ethics. Obviously some of the elements of Abimelech's code of ethics would not be acceptable today. For instance, he took a woman to be his concubine, and he did it against her will. Is there a loophole here for us? Is *any* code of ethics acceptable as long as it is self-consistent and conforms to the local culture? That would certainly open a lot of possibilities in today's permissive society. If you are wondering about this, God is already way ahead of you. Look at these verses:

> All the ways of a man are clean in his own sight,
> But the Lord weighs the motives (Proverbs 16:2).
>
> Every man's way is right in his own eyes,
> But the Lord weighs the hearts (Proverbs 21:2).
>
> There is a way which seems right to a man,
> But its end is the way of death (Proverbs 14:12).

The answer is *no*—not just any code of ethics is acceptable. To be a person of integrity, we must conform to the behavior that God desires. The behavior that God desires was summarized by Jesus in the Golden Rule:

> In everything, therefore, treat people the same way you want them to treat you, for this is the Law and the Prophets (Matthew 7:12).

Jimmy Carter, the president of the United States from 1977 to 1980, was elected to that office after campaigning on the promise that he would never lie to the American people. For Jimmy Carter, that was not just a campaign promise. It was an expression of who he was—a man of the highest personal honesty and integrity.

Following his defeat for re-election in 1980 and his subsequent retirement from public office, he established the Carter Center in Atlanta as a place to resolve conflicts. The Carter Center became the springboard for a wide diversity of post-presidential accomplishments. His status as a former president coupled with his widely acknowledged honesty, integrity, and impartiality opened worldwide doors of opportunity for resolving conflicts and advancing human rights, doors that were probably not open to any other individual. Examples include invitations to monitor democratic transition elections in Haiti, Nicaragua, Zambia, Panama, and the West Bank/Gaza. Other examples include stunningly successful negotiations with leaders considered at the time to be outlaws by many in the world community—Daniel Ortega of Nicaragua, Kim Il Sung of North Korea, and General Raoul Cédras of Haiti[1].

Jimmy Carter's highly visible participation in building low-cost housing through Habitat for Humanity, together with his fund-raising efforts and personal endorsements, have been important factors in that organization's success. Habitat for Humanity, aided over the years by countless donors and volunteers, has built thousands of houses for the less fortunate of many nations.

Honesty? President Anwar Sadat of Egypt, shortly before his assassination, wrote in his personal papers that Jimmy Carter was the most honorable person he knew. Integrity? Carter is a man of intense personal integrity that is fully consistent with his unshakable faith in and commitment to Jesus Christ. Success? Jimmy Carter has been successful in ways that no one could ever have foreseen or even imagined. Do I believe that there is a powerful cause-and-effect relationship here? Absolutely!

IS IGNORANCE A VALID EXCUSE?

The book of Proverbs also addresses and rejects the plea of ignorance—the excuse that we do not act with integrity because we do not know that it is required of us.

> If you say, "See, we did not know this,"
> Does He not consider it who weighs the hearts?
> And does He not know it who keeps your soul?
> And will He not render to man according to his
>   work? (Proverbs 24:12).

These scriptures on the importance of integrity are not evidence of God being harsh with us. Rather they are evidence that the Lord is for us, not against us. He wants us to succeed, not to fail; to be safe, not to suffer harm. He wants us to know that some behavior we may think is perfectly acceptable is not at all acceptable to him. He does not want us to proceed blissfully in ignorance toward our own destruction. He wants us to turn to him, learn his ways, and conform to them.

OUR INTEGRITY AFFECTS OUR CHILDREN

We have seen that our integrity is one of the things that will guard us against evil in this world. Did you also know that God promises blessings to our children if we become persons of integrity? It's true. Look at this verse:

A righteous man who walks in his integrity—
How blessed are his sons after him (Proverbs 20:7).

David wrote:

I have been young and now I am old,
Yet I have not seen the righteous forsaken
Or his descendants begging bread (Psalm 37:25).

The Lord told Solomon, David's son:

As for you, if you will walk before Me as your father
David walked, in integrity of heart and uprightness,
doing according to all that I have commanded you
and will keep My statutes and My ordinances, then I
will establish the throne of your kingdom over Israel
forever, just as I promised to your father David, saying,
"You shall not lack a man on the throne of Israel" (1
Kings 9:4–5).

In summary, our behavior is to be based on the Golden
Rule, often quoted as, "Do unto others as you would have
them do unto you." Integrity protects us in our dealings
with others in three specific ways:

1.   It helps build and protect our reputation.
2.   It helps protect us from attempting to deal
      treacherously with others.
3.   It helps protect us from the treacherous deal-
      ings of others.

Being a person of integrity also brings blessings to our
children. Let us *maintain our integrity.*

PLAN OF ACTION

How do we become persons of integrity? First, we must *decide* to conduct ourselves with integrity. After we have made that decision, we then begin to look to the Lord to teach us how to behave. He will use the Bible, other people, and everyday events to teach us. We must also listen carefully to our consciences, which God put within us to help keep us out of trouble. In every circumstance, we must *try to do the right thing*. Don't be afraid of making a mistake. We are not expected to be perfect, just to operate in integrity to the best of our ability. Then the Lord himself will protect us in our dealings with others.

6

HEED WISE COUNSEL

I n this chapter, we examine the sixth of our twelve Keys to Success: **Heed wise counsel**. The premise of this Key to Success is that, in almost any area of expertise, there are those who are wiser and more knowledgeable than we are. They can help us have more successes and fewer failures than we would have if we did everything on our own. We should seek out and listen carefully to wise counsel before making our final decisions on any major courses of action. We should remain open to wise counsel and instruction from others so that we may increase our knowledge, wisdom, and effectiveness in every area of our lives.

Let us begin by looking at four scriptures from the book of Proverbs:

> The way of a fool is right in his own eyes,
> But a wise man is he who listens to counsel
>   (Proverbs 12:15).

> Without consultation, plans are frustrated,
> But with many counselors they succeed
>   (Proverbs 15:22).

> Prepare plans by consultation,
> And make war by wise guidance (Proverbs 20:18).

> For by wise guidance you will wage war,
> And in abundance of counselors there is victory
>   (Proverbs 24:6).

There is a progression of thought in these verses. The first line of Proverbs 12:15 introduces a person who thinks he or she is always right. A person with this attitude is unwilling to listen to anyone else. The Bible is not very kind: it calls such a person a *fool*. In contrast, the second line of the verse characterizes someone as *wise* who listens to the counsel of others.

PLANS

In the first line of Proverbs 15:22, this person's plans were thwarted, perhaps by opponents, or perhaps by unforeseen circumstances. The second line says that wise counselors would have found ways to modify and adapt the plans so that they would have succeeded.

Proverbs 20:18 focuses on waging a war. However, it also applies to conducting business. A war involves opposing armies, each consisting of a large number of people. If the leadership of an army is wise, the leadership will involve its very best people in the planning process to maximize its chances of victory. The planning process includes determining the objectives, assessing the opposition, generating the strategy to achieve the objectives, defining the organizational structure, planning the training, planning for acquiring the necessary supplies and transporting them to where they will be needed, setting the schedule, deciding on the battle tactics, making contingency plans, and so on.

Assume that the other army has done this planning and preparation, and that now we must fight them. The parallel between war and business strategy should be obvious. How should we proceed? Should we just go out and start fighting, hoping that by some miracle we will be successful against a fully prepared opponent? God does not recommend that course of action. Proverbs 20:18 says that before we make war, before we make that business or career move, we need effective and well-thought-out plans to maximize our chances for success.

I have often been the project director for high-tech, one-of-a-kind developments. When I faced a key technical decision, one that could affect the success of the project, I normally convened a brainstorming meeting of the people working on the project, plus others who had a stake in its success. We openly discussed the issues, proposed solutions, and discussed their pros and cons. In most cases we arrived at a consensus agreement about the best choice. When we didn't reach consensus, it was my job to consider all the information that had been offered, make a decision, and accept the responsibility for that decision.

EXECUTION

Good plans are essential, but a war is not won by good plans. A war is won by successful execution of good plans. That is why Proverbs 24:6 is important. That verse tells us that we also need wise counselors and guidance while we are waging the war because no set of plans is 100 percent accurate. No set of plans is complete enough to handle all possible contingencies. While we are waging war or while we are executing a business or career move, we need wise counselors to help us address the unpredictable events that inevitably occur. In my experience, another meeting of the project personnel and the other stakeholders almost always resulted in a consensus recommendation of the right course of action to take.

God wants to help us achieve victories in our businesses, in our careers, and in our personal lives. One of the Keys to Success that will help us immensely is: **Heed wise counsel**.

THE LORD AS OUR COUNSELOR

Who better could there be to provide wise counsel to us than the Lord, the One who is the source of all wisdom and knowledge? Notice what these next three verses say about the Lord's counsel:

> Many plans are in a man's heart,
> But the counsel of the Lord will stand
>   (Proverbs 19:21).

> The mind of man plans his way,
> But the Lord directs his steps (Proverbs 16:9).

> Who is the man who fears the Lord?
> He will instruct him in the way he should choose
>   (Psalm 25:12).

These verses tell us that the Lord wants to give us wise counsel, to put his plans into our hearts, and to direct our steps onto the path of success. When we have decisions to make, he wants to show us the right choices. And he will show them to us if we will let him.

In making important career or personal decisions, my wife and I begin by discussing and writing down the alternatives and the pros and cons of each choice. By the time we have finished doing that, the answer is often obvious to us. But it might be that the answer that seems best to us is not the one the Lord knows is *really* the best one. A technique that has helped us align our choice with the Lord's choice is as follows. We *decide* to do our first choice, but we take no action for twenty-four to forty-eight hours. We pray for his guidance with our decision. At the end of that time, we will both have an inner peace from the Lord if it is what he wants. If we do not have that inner peace, we decide on a different choice and repeat the test. In the event that none of the possible choices results in an inner peace from the Lord, we maintain the status quo and take no action. We conclude that either it is not the right time to act or that there must be a better choice that we will discover later.

Our Associates

The people with whom we associate can influence our thoughts and attitudes. This influence can in turn affect our actions, and our actions affect our success. Several verses in Proverbs explain how our associates can affect us:

> A fool does not delight in understanding,
> But only in revealing his own mind (Proverbs 18:2).

> Leave the presence of a fool,
> Or you will not discern words of knowledge
>   (Proverbs 14:7).

> He who walks with wise men will be wise,
> But the companion of fools will suffer harm
>   (Proverbs 13:20).

These verses are not addressing moral corruption. They are addressing being influenced by those whom the Bible calls "fools." Proverbs 12:15, which we looked at earlier in this chapter, says a fool thinks he is always right; therefore he will not listen to wise counsel.

Proverbs 18:2 says that whatever we may hear from a fool is worthless. The things he speaks are not based on an understanding of the way things really are. He is simply "speaking his own mind," and there is nothing in there worth hearing. In Proverbs 14:7 we are warned that if we associate with fools and listen to their opinions, we can lose the ability to discern between what is accurate and what is not. Proverbs 13:20 says companionship with fools will cause us harm. It counsels us instead to associate with wise people, to walk with wise people, and to spend our time with wise people. That way, we may also become wise.

There are a number of verses in the book of Proverbs that tell us wisdom is to be highly prized, and we should pursue it. For example:

Make your ear attentive to wisdom,
Incline your heart to understanding (Proverbs 2:2).

How blessed is the man who finds wisdom
And the man who gains understanding
    (Proverbs 3:13).

We must be careful to choose associates who can help us receive this blessing of wisdom.

CORRECTION

Earlier in the chapter, we spoke of seeking wise counselors who could help us make and execute plans. Suppose we did not do this and are now in trouble. What should we do? Very simply, we should start from where we are, get help from wise counselors, and move on toward victory over the present trouble. Although this course of action sounds simple, there are real obstacles in many people's attitudes that keep them from doing it. The two primary obstacles are their belief that they are always right and their refusal to accept what the book of Proverbs calls *reproof.* Reproof is friendly correction intended to help us overcome a fault. None of us like to be corrected or to be told that we have a fault that we need to overcome. However, the fact that we may not *like* reproof is irrelevant. God never asks us to like it, but he does tell us to accept it, heed it, and act on it. If we will do that, it will lead us on toward success. If we do not, it can lead to our ruin.

Instruction and reproof are tightly coupled aspects of learning. Instruction tells us the way we should do something. Reproof explains how we have been doing it wrong and admonishes us to do it the right way. Look at what the Bible says can happen to a person who refuses to listen to instruction and who refuses reproof:

> And you say, "How I have hated instruction!
> And my heart spurned reproof!
> I have not listened to the voice of my teachers,
> Nor inclined my ear to my instructors!
> I was almost in utter ruin
> In the midst of the assembly and congregation"
>> (Proverbs 5:12–14).

The stubborn attitude of the person being described in refusing instruction and correction brought him to the point of utter ruin before he realized what he was doing. Other verses in the book of Proverbs encourage us to be teachable and to accept correction:

> He is on the path of life who heeds instruction,
> But he who ignores reproof goes astray
>> (Proverbs 10:17).

> Poverty and shame will come to him who neglects discipline,
> But he who regards reproof will be honored
>> (Proverbs 13:18).

> He whose ear listens to the life-giving reproof
> Will dwell among the wise.
> He who neglects discipline despises himself,
> But he who listens to reproof acquires understanding
>   (Proverbs 15:31–32).

God wants us to learn to accept and act on guidance, instruction, and correction. It may come from our counselors, our spouses, our friends, our peers, or our bosses. God himself is also our Counselor, our Friend, and our King. He wants us to learn to accept and act on his instructions and reproof so that he can help us succeed.

> My son, do not reject the discipline of the Lord
> Or loathe His reproof,
> For whom the Lord loves He reproves,
> Even as a father corrects the son in whom he delights
>   (Proverbs 3:11–12).

> Listen to counsel and accept discipline,
> That you may be wise the rest of your days
>   (Proverbs 19:20).

Psalm 25 says that one purpose of the Lord's instruction and correction is to bring prosperity to us and to our children.

> Who is the man who fears the Lord?
> He will instruct him in the way he should choose.
> His soul will abide in prosperity,
> And his descendants will inherit the land
>   (Psalm 25:12–13).

PLAN OF ACTION

There are three things we must do to *heed wise counsel*, our sixth Key to Success. First, we must seek out and listen to wise counselors who can help us develop and execute our plans. This especially includes seeking the Lord's guidance. Second, we must be careful whom we choose for our associates. We should spend our time with those who are wise and avoid those whom the Bible calls fools. Third, we must learn to accept instruction and correction and act on them.

7

BE DILIGENT

The next Key to Success that we will look at is: **Be diligent**. A diligent person is industrious, persevering, hardworking, and thorough. Two words that characterize someone who is the opposite of a diligent person are lazy and sluggard. A lazy person lacks ambition and is disinclined to work. A sluggard is apathetic, slow-moving, and unwilling to work. We will see these words used repeatedly in the verses we study in this chapter.

The diligent and the sluggard are at the opposite ends of a spectrum of attitudes toward work. At the productive end of the spectrum is the diligent person. He is industrious and works intensely and persistently toward accomplishing his goals. At the other end of the spectrum is the sluggard, whose primary aim is to avoid work. Common sense tells us that diligence will help us succeed and that laziness will lead us to failure.

God concurs with what common sense tells us about diligence and laziness. He provides many scriptures in the book of Proverbs that contrast the actions and the end result of the diligent with the actions and the end result of the sluggard. He does this because he wants us to succeed, not to fail, and it is important that we understand this aspect of our responsibility in achieving the success he desires for us.

Notice this description of a sluggard:

> I passed by the field of the sluggard
> And by the vineyard of the man lacking sense,

> And behold, it was completely overgrown with
>   thistles;
> Its surface was covered with nettles,
> And its stone wall was broken down.
> When I saw, I reflected upon it;
> I looked, and received instruction.
> "A little sleep, a little slumber,
> A little folding of the hands to rest,"
> Then your poverty will come as a robber
> And your want like an armed man
>   (Proverbs 24:30–34).

We have here the image of someone who is wasting all of his resources. The reasons are laziness, apathy, and unwillingness to work. He spends his time sleeping instead of working.

Notice that he has a field in which he could be growing crops to feed himself and his family, to maintain livestock, and to sell as a cash crop. He also has a vineyard that could be producing grapes for wine and raisins. At one time there was an intact wall around the property. The wall would have served to keep livestock in their pasture. It would also have served to keep livestock out of the vineyard and away from the other crops. This man has adequate resources available to provide well for himself and his family. He is just too lazy to make use of them.

How did a sluggard get such resources in the first place? The Bible doesn't tell us. Perhaps he inherited them from his parents or grandparents. If so, they or their parents before them must have worked hard, building up the farm, clearing the rocks from the fields and using them to build the protective stone walls. They must have planted and tended the grapevines. Proverbs 13:22a says, "A good man leaves an inheritance to his children's children." Upon the death of his parents, this man would have become the owner.

Another possibility is that the man himself had once been diligent. Perhaps in earlier times he had tilled and planted the field, growing, harvesting, and selling the crops. Perhaps he had raised livestock, tended the vineyard, and harvested and sold its fruit. He had maintained the stone wall to protect his crops and to contain his livestock. But then something happened that caused him to lose interest in the property and become lazy. He began to indulge himself in resting and sleeping, instead of in working.

Whatever the cause, his laziness has progressed to the point that the Bible labels him a sluggard. The protective wall around his property is broken down in a number of places because of his neglect. His fields and his vineyard are completely overgrown with thistles and nettles. Even if there were some untended produce growing on his property—grain in the field, grapes in the vineyard—it could not be harvested. The thistles and the nettles growing there would make it impossible to get to the crop. The property that once was valuable is now practically worthless. The results are no different than if a thief or a robber had taken everything that the man had. The cause might be different, but the results would be the same.

In the next few scriptures, God further emphasizes the dangers of resting and sleeping when we should be working:

> Laziness casts into a deep sleep,
> And an idle man will suffer hunger (Proverbs 19:15).

> Do not love sleep, or you will become poor;
> Open your eyes, and you will be satisfied with food
>   (Proverbs 20:13).

And this humorous description:

> As the door turns on its hinges,
> So does the sluggard on his bed (Proverbs 26:14).

For some people, even if success were so close that all they would have to do is reach out and pull it in, they have become too lazy and unmotivated to do even that. The situation is described in the book of Proverbs in this way:

> The sluggard buries his hand in the dish,
> But will not even bring it back to his mouth
>   (Proverbs 19:24).

> The sluggard buries his hand in the dish;
> He is weary of bringing it to his mouth again
>   (Proverbs 26:15).

The book of Proverbs asks:

> How long will you lie down, O sluggard?
> When will you arise from your sleep?
> "A little sleep, a little slumber,
> A little folding of the hands to rest" —
> Your poverty will come in like a vagabond
> And your need like an armed man (Proverbs 6:9–11).

Why do we become lazy? What has demotivated us? What has immobilized us? There may or may not be simple answers to these questions. Nevertheless, the *solution* to the problem is clearly prescribed in the verses that immediately precede the previous passage:

> Go to the ant, O sluggard,
> Observe her ways and be wise,
> Which, having no chief,

> Officer or ruler,
> Prepares her food in the summer
> And gathers her provision in the harvest
>   (Proverbs 6:6–8).

There are four steps to recovery outlined here: 1) Recognize our condition; 2) Find out what we must change; 3) Start doing it; and 4) Keep on doing it.

Step 1. Recognize our condition.

O sluggard. There is a broad range of possibilities, from the pure sluggard to the person who is 100 percent diligent. If we picture the sluggard on one end of a line and the diligent on the other, most of us are somewhere between the two extremes. Our first step toward improving is to conduct a truthful assessment of ourselves to determine where we are along that line: for instance, 30 percent sluggard and 70 percent diligent. In conducting this assessment, it is very important to be truthful with ourselves and with God. He already knows, but it is important for *us* to know because Jesus said:

> And you will know the truth, and the truth will make you free (John 8:32).

The closer we are to the diligent end of that line, the more likely we are to succeed. The closer we are to the sluggard end of the line, the more we will need to correct our attitudes toward work if we desire to be successful. We will also need to recognize and assess any reluctance we may have toward changing our attitudes and our behavior. Once we have honestly assessed our level of diligence, we are ready for the next step.

Step 2. Find out what we must change.

Go to the ant, observe her ways, and be wise. There are solutions; it is our responsibility to look for them. We can begin by asking ourselves what specific things we could do to increase our diligence.

Which, having no chief, officer or ruler. Ants are self–motivated. They have no need of anyone to force them to work.

Prepares her food in the summer and gathers her provisions in the harvest. Ants do what they must do to provide for the future. They take advantage of the opportunities when they exist.

If we have assessed our condition and want to change but don't know what to do next, we should seek out wise counselors who can help us get started. It's kind of like one of those light bulb jokes:

Question: How many psychiatrists does it take to change a light bulb?

Answer: Only one—but the light bulb really has to want to change.

Others can help us identify the actions to take, but it is our responsibility to take those actions.

Step 3. Start doing it.

Once we have defined the course of action and made the decision to do it, then we must start. We must get busy! We must do it! If we have determined that we are not sufficiently diligent, then we need to recognize that our lack of diligence will make it even harder for us to get started. This is all the more reason to get started quickly. We don't want to be like the fellow who knew he needed to join Procrastinators Anonymous but could never seem to get around to doing it. Let us set a definite date and time to start, and hold to it.

Step 4. Keep on doing it.

If the lack of sufficient diligence is a problem for us, it may be difficult to break that pattern. It may take a concerted and persistent effort on our part to apply ourselves more diligently. To be diligent is to be industrious, persevering, hardworking, and thorough. As we begin to develop diligence as part of our character, over time we will need less and less conscious effort to keep on being diligent. Of course, there will still be times when we must make ourselves be persistent in working toward our goals. When times like that are at hand, we can apply the words of the Apostle Paul as we face the temptation to slack off:

> Brethren, I do not regard myself as having laid hold of it yet; but one thing I do: forgetting what lies behind and reaching forward to what lies ahead, I press on toward the goal for the prize of the upward call of God in Christ Jesus. Let us therefore, as many as are perfect, have this attitude; and if in anything you have a different attitude, God will reveal that also to you; however, let us keep living by that same standard to which we have attained (Philippians 3:13–16).

PLAN OF ACTION

God wants us to succeed. He points out that one of the great dangers to our success is a lack of sufficient diligence toward our work. There are four steps by which we can address and overcome the lack of diligence in our lives:

1. Recognize our condition.
2. Find out what we must change.
3. Start doing it.
4. Keep on doing it.

8

TREAT EVERYONE
WITH RESPECT

It is intuitive to most people in business that they should treat their customers with respect—fairly, honestly, with recognition of their worth, and with genuine concern for their well-being—for without sufficient purchases from its customers, no business can succeed. It should also be intuitive that a business should treat its employees with respect—fairly, honestly, with recognition of their worth, and with genuine concern for their well-being—for without the efforts of its employees, no business can succeed. It is probably less intuitive that a business should also treat its suppliers with respect—for without good suppliers, no business can succeed. A truly successful business strives to find and keep good customers. It strives to find and keep good employees. And it strives to find and keep good suppliers.

This chapter discusses the Key to Success that says: **Treat everyone with respect**. While this applies very broadly—to parents, spouse, children, friends, coworkers, etc.—we will focus our study on how to treat employees. Many wise sayings in the book of Proverbs apply directly to how business owners, managers, and supervisors should treat their employees. As we come to understand and practice God's counsel in this area, we will experience more success in our businesses and our careers.

I am not, nor have I ever been, an owner of a business. I have been an employee throughout my career. However, I have often also been responsible for some of the other employees of the businesses where I have worked, as their manager or supervisor. Some of the scriptures we will study apply only to the owner of a business, but most of them also apply to me and to others like me who manage or supervise employees.

There are some businesses that are so small that they are operated solely by the owner and have no other employees. I heard about a street vendor in a large city who sold hot dogs to the lunch crowd. One day one of his customers said, "You know, you sell great hot dogs, but don't you think five dollars is too much to charge for one?" The vendor replied, "Yes it is, but let me tell you how it happened. When I started in business, I sold my hot dogs for a dollar apiece. My business grew until I could no longer serve all my customers by myself. I didn't want the headaches of having other employees, so I just raised my prices. Since then, every time my business grows to the point where I can no longer handle it by myself, I raise my prices. That's why I charge five dollars for a hot dog."

Well, it may have worked for that hot dog vendor, but most people cannot run a successful business without having employees. As the sales grow, there is a corresponding need to add employees. Because God wants us to be successful, and because our employees can very strongly affect the success of our businesses or careers, he has a number of things to say about the kinds of people to hire and how to treat them. Let's begin by looking at an unusual verse:

> Where no oxen are, the manger is clean,
> But much revenue comes by the strength of the ox
> (Proverbs 14:4).

An ox is a huge, powerful animal. A team of oxen was used in biblical days—and even in Colonial America and the American West—to pull a plow, pull a wagon, or drag heavy objects. The ox was a tremendous force multiplier for a farmer. By using a team of oxen, a farmer could cultivate many times the acreage that would be possible using just a hoe, a shovel, and a hand plow. A team of oxen could pull an entire wagon full of grain to market. They could be used to help clear stumps and large rocks from a new field. It is obvious that, for a farmer, "much revenue comes by the strength of the ox." But this revenue is not free. The farmer has to buy the oxen. He also has to buy or build a yoke, a plow, and a wagon to make optimum use of the oxen. He has to feed and water them, and he needs a barn to protect them from bad weather. If he separates each ox in its own stall, the remainder of the barn can be used to store tools, food for the oxen, seed, and last year's crops.

A byproduct of having oxen is that there is a large amount of urine and manure that must be regularly cleaned out of each stall. Otherwise, not only will the barn smell bad, but the oxen's feet can become infected so that they are unable to work.

I want you to clearly see the picture here. The more oxen there are and the bigger the oxen are, the more manure there is to shovel out of the stalls. Therefore, part of the price of keeping oxen is to handle all the manure that they regularly produce. While he's shoveling manure, it is important that the farmer keeps things in perspective: no oxen, no manure to shovel, but "much revenue comes by the strength of the ox." Can you see the analogy between a biblical farmer's oxen and your employees? Having employees is a lot more trouble than not having them, but a business can be much more successful and therefore make significantly more money if it can *make effective use of good employees.*

HIRE GOOD EMPLOYEES

Let's look in more detail at this idea: *Make effective use of good employees.* The process begins by hiring people who are, or have the traits to become, good employees. Depending on where we work, hiring may be from the outside, or it may mean negotiating for people from within the company labor pool. What are the traits that make for good employees? The key ones are these:

- Competence
- Initiative
- Diligence
- Honesty
- Cooperative attitude

Many people have traits that prevent them from being desirable employees. The Lord does not propose that we hire such people. In fact, he warns us against hiring several specific types of people and advises us to get rid of some categories of people if we are already employing them. Why? It is because he wants us to succeed. Having bad employees is a detriment to the success of any enterprise. Obviously, we must not be an undesirable type of employee ourselves!

In the same way that God wants *us* to "lay aside the old self...and put on the new self" (Ephesians 4:22–24), he wants every other person to also do this. For this reason, in evaluating a person as a prospective employee, we should focus on determining the kind of person he or she is *now* and give less emphasis to what he or she was like formerly. Some people change for the better over time; others change for the worse.

What kinds of people should we avoid hiring? We should not hire the lazy.

> Like vinegar to the teeth and smoke to the eyes,
> So is the lazy one to those who send him
>   (Proverbs 10:26).

We should not hire the undependable.

> Like a bad tooth and an unsteady foot
> Is confidence in a faithless man in time of trouble
>   (Proverbs 25:19).

We should not hire the foolish.

> He cuts off his own feet and drinks violence
> Who sends a message by the hand of a fool
>   (Proverbs 26:6).

We should not hire someone lacking initiative or someone who will be unresponsive to instructions.

> A slave will not be instructed by words alone;
> For though he understands, there will be no response
>   (Proverbs 29:19).

We should not hire someone who behaves indecently.

> The king's favor is toward a servant who acts wisely,
> But his anger is toward him who acts shamefully
>   (Proverbs 14:35).

We should not hire someone who would take advantage of the poor.

> He who oppresses the poor taunts his Maker,
> But he who is gracious to the needy honors Him
>   (Proverbs 14:31).

We should not hire someone with a violent temper.

> Do not associate with a man given to anger;
> Or go with a hot-tempered man,
> Or you will learn his ways
> And find a snare for yourself (Proverbs 22:24–25).

> A man of great anger will bear the penalty,
> For if you rescue him, you will only have to do it
>   again (Proverbs 19:19).

We should not hire a quarrelsome person or a person who would cause strife with the customers, the suppliers, or among the other employees.

> Keeping away from strife is an honor for a man,
> But any fool will quarrel (Proverbs 20:3).

> Like charcoal to hot embers and wood to fire,
> So is a contentious man to kindle strife
>   (Proverbs 26:21).

We should not hire a gossip or a slanderer.

> A perverse man spreads strife,
> And a slanderer separates intimate friends
>   (Proverbs 16:28).

> He who goes about as a slanderer reveals secrets,
> Therefore do not associate with a gossip
>   (Proverbs 20:19).

The Lord puts the responsibility for who we hire squarely upon our shoulders. We must therefore *be very careful whom we hire.*

> Like an archer who wounds everyone,
> So is he who hires a fool or who hires those who pass
>   by (Proverbs 26:10).

Hiring good employees will bring blessings to our businesses and to our careers. Having bad employees will affect both of these negatively in several ways:

- Poor productivity from bad employees costs money.
- An employee's poor attitude toward customers can lose customers and sales.
- An employee's negative attitude and poor work habits can hurt the performance and attitude of other employees.

What is the solution when we recognize that we have made a mistake and hired a bad employee? It is the kind and merciful thing to try to reform him or her, and sometimes that will succeed. However, the Lord does not *require* us to try to reform but rather advises us to get rid of such a one. Then we should try to learn from our hiring mistake so that we will be less likely to repeat it.

> For lack of wood the fire goes out,
> And where there is no whisperer, contention quiets
>   down (Proverbs 26:20).

> Drive out the scoffer, and contention will go out,
> Even strife and dishonor will cease (Proverbs 22:10).

TREAT EMPLOYEES JUSTLY

When employees perceive that they are being dealt with justly, it has a very positive effect on their motivation and their attitude toward their work. It is very important to the success of our businesses and our careers to *treat our employees justly*. To be just is to be impartial, objective, and fair. Note the following verses about being just.

> He who justifies the wicked and he who condemns
>   the righteous,
> Both of them alike are an abomination to the Lord
>   (Proverbs 17:15).

> To show partiality to the wicked is not good,
> Nor to thrust aside the righteous in judgment
>   (Proverbs 18:5).

> The exercise of justice is joy for the righteous,
> But is terror to the workers of iniquity
>   (Proverbs 21:15).

> When the righteous increase, the people rejoice,
> But when a wicked man rules, people groan
>   (Proverbs 29:2).

In evaluating a situation involving an employee, we must guard against prematurely jumping to erroneous conclusions. We should begin by trying to understand all of the pertinent facts, being sure to listen with an open mind to each person involved or affected. To the best of our ability, we should ferret out the full truth before making a decision on the issue. Here are two scriptures that directly address this process.

> He who gives an answer before he hears,
> It is folly and shame to him (Proverbs 18:13).

> The first to plead his case seems right,
> Until another comes and examines him
>   (Proverbs 18:17).

In the first verse, God counsels us to learn all the pertinent facts to the best of our abilities before we make a decision. In the second verse, he addresses the case of a disagreement or dispute between two people. He cautions us to listen carefully to *both* sides of the issue before drawing a conclusion about who is in the right and who is in the wrong.

BE AN ENCOURAGER

Another way that we can positively affect our employees' attitudes and performance is to be an encourager to them. We encourage them when we compliment them, reassure them, cheer them up, boost their confidence, and inspire their hope.

Our success in our businesses and our careers is strongly affected by how well our employees and associates perform their work. In the same way that diligence is an important trait in ourselves, as we saw in the previous chapter, it is also an important trait for our employees and our associates to have. We can encourage diligence in others not only by what we say but also by what we model in our own behavior.

It is much easier for people to work well when they are sufficiently rested and in good health. It is much more difficult to work well when we are tired or ill. It is part of our role to advocate that all take care of their health and try as much as possible to provide employees with the means and the opportunities to do so.

It is also much more difficult for people to work well when they are worried, anxious, hurting emotionally, or suffering from what the Bible calls a broken spirit. Preventing discouragement is much easier than overcoming it. And it is much easier to help those who are simply feeling discouraged than to help them after their discouragement has progressed to dejection, depression, despondency, or despair. The Bible describes it like this:

> A joyful heart makes a cheerful face,
> But when the heart is sad, the spirit is broken
>   (Proverbs 15:13).

> A joyful heart is good medicine,
> But a broken spirit dries up the bones
>   (Proverbs 17:22).

> The spirit of a man can endure his sickness,
> But as for a broken spirit who can bear it? (Proverbs
>   18:14).

The easiest way to help prevent discouragement is to foster a joyful, positive, and upbeat work atmosphere, and to *be an encourager.*

> A man has joy in an apt answer,
> And how delightful is a timely word!
>   (Proverbs 15:23).

> Pleasant words are a honeycomb,
> Sweet to the soul and healing to the bones
>   (Proverbs 16:24).

We are responsible to God for our employees, even as a shepherd is responsible to the owner for the sheep under his care. We should continually try to lift up people's spirits and boost their joy by speaking a good word of faith and encouragement.

> Anxiety in a man's heart weighs it down,
> But a good word makes it glad (Proverbs 12:25).

> Hope deferred makes the heart sick,
> But desire fulfilled is a tree of life (Proverbs 13:12).
>
> Desire realized is sweet to the soul (Proverbs 13:19a).

Earlier in the chapter we noted a similarity between a modern-day employer and a biblical farmer. To continue that analogy:

> Know well the condition of your flocks,
> And pay attention to your herds;
> For riches are not forever,
> Nor does a crown endure to all generations.
> When the grass disappears, the new growth is seen,
> And the herbs of the mountains are gathered in,
> The lambs will be for your clothing,
> And the goats will bring the price of a field,
> And there will be goats' milk enough for your food,
> For the food of your household,
> And sustenance for your maidens
> (Proverbs 27:23–27).

Thus the Bible says it is important to our success to keep a loving, watchful eye over our employees. Their condition affects not only the work they are currently doing, but it also affects the future success of the business.

SHARE THE SUCCESSES

Before we conclude the analogy with the biblical farmer, let us look at one of the seemingly unusual laws that God gave the people of Israel.

> You shall not muzzle the ox while he is threshing
>   (Deuteronomy 25:4).

There is no surrounding context for this verse to help us understand its importance. We must turn to the New Testament where the Apostle Paul uses it in his first letter to the church at Corinth to find out what it really means.

> Who at any time serves as a soldier at his own expense? Who plants a vineyard and does not eat the fruit of it? Or who tends a flock and does not use the milk of the flock?
>   I am not speaking these things according to human judgment, am I? Or does not the Law also say these things? For it is written in the Law of Moses, "You shall not muzzle the ox while he is threshing." God is not concerned about oxen, is He? Or is He speaking altogether for our sake? Yes, for our sake it was written, because the plowman ought to plow in hope, and the thresher to thresh in hope of sharing the crops (1 Corinthians 9:7–10).

This scripture is directly addressing the way employees are compensated. They are to be paid for the job they are doing and are also to be provided with the equipment and supplies they need: "Who at any time serves as a soldier at his own expense?" Then the verse continues by discussing some employee "perks." It says that it is expected that the person who tends the vineyard can eat some of its grapes, and the shepherd can drink some of the milk from the flock. Note, however, that this is for personal consumption and does not extend to an employee selling these products and keeping the proceeds. Similarly, the ox that is treading out the grain must not be forbidden from eating some of it.

On the surface, these perks appear to cost a business extra money. It seems like the associated expenses would cut into the business profits. The last verse explains why that is not true. That verse says that employees ought to work *in hope* of sharing the crops, in hope of sharing in the success of each business year. There are two implications here. The first is that employees will be better employees, happier employees, harder working and more productive employees if they believe that they will be sharing in the business successes. The second implication is that the business will net more income in the end if its employees are so motivated. We are to *share the successes* with our employees.

PLAN OF ACTION

We should review the employment practices where we work and define the kinds of employees we want working for us. We should then assess both the positive and the negative traits in our current employees. Next, we should develop a plan for reforming or replacing our undesirable employees. Because of government labor laws, we should submit this plan to wise counsel before implementing it.

We should try to find out the degree to which our employees view us as being just. Then we need to develop a plan to improve our performance in this area.

We need to become encouragers to our employees and our associates. We can seek advice on ways to do this from people who are already effective encouragers.

We should re-examine our employee compensation policies, looking specifically for ways to motivate our employees through sharing the success of the business with them.

9

HANDLE MONEY WISELY

I n this chapter, we will be looking at what God has to say in several areas that relate to how we handle money, both in our businesses and in our personal lives. Specifically we will address paying creditors, cosigning notes, saving, and giving. This Key to Success is: **Handle money wisely.**

PAY CREDITORS PROMPTLY

God is very clear and concise when it comes to the matter of paying our bills: we are to pay them, and do it as promptly as we can.

> Do not withhold good from those to whom it is due,
> When it is in your power to do it.
> Do not say to your neighbor, "Go, and come back,
> And tomorrow I will give it,"
> When you have it with you (Proverbs 3:27–28).

Note that this scripture does not approve of the practice of holding off as long as possible on paying either our business or our personal accounts as an interest-free means to finance our cash flow.

DO NOT COSIGN NOTES

God is also very clear about the matter of cosigning a promissory note. He warns us not to do it unless we are both willing and able to pay the full amount of the note. In the following verses, a guarantor is someone who is legally liable for another person's debt if he or she defaults. One place where such obligations can arise is within a business partnership agreement.

A man lacking in sense pledges
And becomes guarantor in the presence of his
    neighbor (Proverbs 17:18).

He who is guarantor for a stranger will surely suffer
    for it,
But he who hates being a guarnator is secure.
    (Proverbs 11:15).

Do not be among those who give pledges,
Among those who become guarantors for debts.
If you have nothing with which to pay,
Why should he take your bed from under you?
    (Proverbs 22:26–27).

What should we do if we became obligated in this way before we learned what God has to say? The answer is to get released from the agreement as quickly as possible, before we suffer (more) serious financial harm.

My son, if you have become surety for your neighbor,
Have given a pledge for a stranger,
If you have been snared with the words of your
    mouth,
Have been caught with the words of your mouth,
Do this then, my son, and deliver yourself;
Since you have come into the hand of your neighbor,
Go, humble yourself, and importune your neighbor.
Give no sleep to your eyes,
Nor slumber to your eyelids;

Deliver yourself like a gazelle from the hunter's hand
And like a bird from the hand of the fowler
(Proverbs 6:1–5).

SAVE

The premise behind the need to save is that neither our income nor our expenses accrue uniformly throughout our lives. If we spend all of our available income so that we do not have sufficient cash reserves, then when our income suddenly drops because of

- sickness,
- a cutback in our working hours,
- a slow sales period that reduces our commission income,
- loss of our job,

or when our expenses are increased by such events as

- medical needs,
- a new baby,
- braces for a child's teeth,
- house repairs,
- car repairs,
- college for a child,
- going back to school ourselves,
- helping a family member,

we can almost immediately be *plunged into debt*. How deeply into debt we go depends on how severe the financial drain is and how long it lasts. The preventative to falling into debt at the slightest adverse circumstances is to have sufficient cash reserves to draw upon.

A familiar expression that refers to understanding a simple concept is, "It doesn't take a rocket scientist to know that..." Coincidentally, I have been a rocket scientist. I have worked on the design, modeling, or testing of several missile systems during my career. It doesn't take a rocket scientist to understand the mathematics of saving money:

Money available for saving =
Current income − Current outflow

In order to *save*, our *current outflow* of money must be smaller than our *current income*. Current outflow consists of expenditures that are absolutely necessary, plus our optional expenditures. Let us assume that our income and outflow are equal. We would not be saving money, but we would not be going into debt. We would have money available to save if we can do any of the following:

- Increase our income while holding our expenditures constant.
- Reduce our expenditures while holding our income constant.
- Increase our income but increase our expenditures less.
- Reduce our income, but reduce our expenditures more.

We can try to increase our income by a number of strategies:

- Seek a higher paying job within our field.
- Go to school and train for a higher paying job, either in our field or in a different career.

- Become a better employee so that we can earn better raises.
- Work harder and more effectively so that we can increase our sales commissions.
- Take a second job.
- Have others in the family take a job.

A key to reducing expenditures is to first categorize them into necessary versus optional expenditures. Stated another way, what do we absolutely have to spend to be able to stay alive and healthy, eat regularly, sleep indoors, and remain employed? These are our necessary expenses. Almost everything else we spend is an optional expenditure. Our optional expenditures are most often targeted at increasing our creature comforts and enjoyment of life, or improving the way others view us or how we feel about ourselves. As we prayerfully submit all of these money-related issues to the Lord—our income, our essential expenditures, and our optional expenditures—he will help us understand how to achieve a balance that is wise, beneficial to us, and pleasing to him.

Definitions of *not being in debt* range from being current on all of our bills and payments to not owing anything on a credit card, to not having any money borrowed from anyone for any reason. Personally, I have borrowed money whenever I have bought a house or a car. I do not normally buy appliances, television sets, personal computers, furniture, or the like on credit. I first save the money and then pay cash for them. I also do not borrow money on my credit cards. I use them but normally pay off the full balance each month. If I cannot pay cash for an item, I try to do without it.

To *get out of debt*, we must increase our income and/or reduce our expenditures. Then we use the money we save to pay off our current bills first, our credit cards next, and then the remainder of our debts (cars, house). Especially when times are good and our income is high, we must be wise enough to take advantage of the good times by voluntarily restricting our expenditures, paying down our debts, and accumulating cash reserves for when times may not be so good. To *stay out of debt*, we must build up our cash reserves so we can handle the known and the unexpected expenses that will occur.

In Genesis 41, God warned Pharaoh in a dream that there were going to be seven years of plentiful harvests in Egypt. Immediately following them would be seven very lean years in which the crops would be inadequate. God then gave Joseph a plan for the way to prepare for the years ahead. The plan was to save and store 20 percent of the crop in each of the seven plentiful years. That reserve would then be used to supplement the food supply in the seven lean years that would follow. In that way, the nation would survive. Joseph, in implementing this plan on behalf of the Pharaoh, saved not only the nation of Egypt, he also saved his wife and children, his father, his brothers and their families, and therefore the entire future nation of Israel.

In the book of Proverbs, the Lord points out the ant as an example of one who wisely works and saves during the advantageous times.

> The ant...prepares her food in the summer
> And gathers her provision in the harvest
>   (Proverbs 6:6a, 8).

> Four things are small on the earth,
> But they are exceedingly wise:
> The ants are not a strong people,
> But they prepare their food in the summer
>   (Proverbs 30:24–25).

The Lord speaks of the unconstrained consumer in this way:

> He who loves pleasure will become a poor man;
> He who loves wine and oil will not become rich
>   (Proverbs 21:17).

He contrasts the lifestyle of the saver (the wise) with that of the excessive consumer (the foolish) in this way:

> There is precious treasure and oil in the dwelling of
>   the wise,
> But a foolish man swallows it up (Proverbs 21:20).

Finally, he contrasts the results of saving with the results of excessive consumption:

> The rich rules over the poor,
> And the borrower becomes the lender's slave
>   (Proverbs 22:7).

GIVE

The book of Proverbs has this to say about people who give:

> There is one who scatters, and yet increases all the more,
> And there is one who withholds what is justly due,
>   and yet it results only in want.
> The generous man will be prosperous,
> And he who waters will himself be watered
>   (Proverbs 11:24–25).

These verses point out the advantages of personal giving and of having an attitude of generosity and giving. They say that we will become more prosperous if we are people who give than if we are not. That certainly goes counter to people's normal way of thinking. The normal way of thinking is, "The more we keep, the more we will have." Let's try God's way on this point and see what happens.

So where should we give?

Don't give to the rich.

> He who oppresses the poor to make more for himself
> Or who gives to the rich, will only come to poverty
> (Proverbs 22:16).

Since poverty is not our goal, let's not oppress the poor, and let's not give to the rich.

Give to God.

> Honor the Lord from your wealth
> And from the first of all your produce;
> So your barns will be filled with plenty
> And your vats will overflow with new wine
> (Proverbs 3:9–10).

This scripture speaks of giving to God from two sources: what we already have (our wealth) and our current income (the first of all our produce). It then declares the benefits of this kind of giving. Rather than diminishing our wealth, the result of giving to the Lord is that our wealth will increase (our barns will be filled) and our income will increase (our vats will overflow). What a glorious promise from God!

Give to the poor.

In this book we have looked at scriptures that assure us that the Lord does not want us to be poor. He warns us again and again not to do those things that will lead to our poverty. In verse after verse he tells us things to do so that we will succeed. But on the other hand, he loves people even though they are poor, and he does not want us to take advantage of or harm those whom he loves. He also does not want us to ignore the poor or be just neutral toward them. Instead, he wants us to be both kind and generous to them. Note these scriptures:

> He who shuts his ear to the cry of the poor
> Will also cry himself and not be answered
>   (Proverbs 21:13).

> He who gives to the poor will never want,
> But he who shuts his eyes will have many curses
>   (Proverbs 28:27).

> He who is generous will be blessed,
> For he gives some of his food to the poor
>   (Proverbs 22:9).

> One who is gracious to a poor man lends to the Lord,
> And He will repay him for his good deed
>   (Proverbs 19:17).

Finally, the Apostle Paul has this to say on the subject of giving as he compares giving to investing wisely in our future:

> Now this I say, he who sows sparingly will also reap sparingly, and he who sows bountifully will also reap bountifully. Each one must do just as he has purposed in his heart, not grudgingly or under compulsion, for God loves a cheerful giver. And God is able to make all grace abound to you, so that always having all sufficiency in everything, you may have an abundance for every good deed; as it is written,
>> "He scattered abroad, he gave to the poor,
>> His righteousness endures forever"
>>   (2 Corinthians 9:6–9).

Paul goes on in the two next verses to tell us that everything we need is available from God. God can give us our start in a business or a career, provide what we need to keep going, and then bless and multiply our efforts. In return, we are to give to his work and to give thanks to him.

> Now He who supplies seed to the sower and bread for food will supply and multiply your seed for sowing and increase the harvest of your righteousness; you will be enriched in everything for all liberality, which through us is producing thanksgiving to God (2 Corinthians 9:10–11).

SUMMARY

We have addressed four topics in this chapter related to handling money wisely:

- Pay creditors promptly.
- Do not cosign notes.
- Save.
- Give.

We conclude this chapter with these words from Paul's first letter to Timothy:

> Instruct those who are rich in this present world not to be conceited or to fix their hope on the uncertainty of riches, but on God, who richly supplies us with all things to enjoy. Instruct them to do good, to be rich in good works, to be generous and ready to share, storing up for themselves the treasure of a good foundation for the future, so that they may take hold of that which is life indeed (1 Timothy 6:17–19).

PLAN OF ACTION

We should develop a plan to pay our creditors promptly, working toward becoming current with all of our bills.

If we have cosigned any notes or if we are in any partnerships, we must evaluate our financial exposure. If we are unwilling or unable to afford the potential losses, we should seek wise counsel on how to extricate ourselves. And we should do this quickly.

To be able to save more, we need to define a plan to reduce our necessary expenditures and cut our optional expenditures. Simultaneously, we should look for ways to increase our income. We should submit our plan to wise counsel before implementing it.

Finally we should define a plan for giving to the Lord and giving to the poor. We should include this plan in our budget but submit the plan to wise counsel before implementing it.

10

BEWARE OF THE LOVE OF MONEY

The thrust of this book up to this point has been to examine biblical Keys to Success that can help us succeed in our businesses, our careers, and our personal lives. Over and over again the message has been that God wants us to succeed and not fail, and this message is true. However, as with any truth in the Bible, it is possible to over-emphasize a message to the point that it becomes distorted and out of proportion to what God intended.

If our definition of success becomes focused upon wealth rather than upon knowing and pleasing God, we have a problem with greed and self-centeredness. A warning light needs to be turned on because we are in danger. *Greed* is an excessive desire for money or possessions. *Self-centeredness* is being overly concerned with ourselves, our desires, and our interests. The Apostle Paul presents a very clear warning against pursuing wealth for its own sake in his first letter to Timothy.

> But those who want to get rich fall into temptation and a snare and many foolish and harmful desires which plunge men into ruin and destruction. For the love of money is a root of all sorts of evil, and some by longing for it have wandered away from the faith and pierced themselves with many griefs. But flee from these things, you man of God, and pursue righteousness, godliness, faith, love, perseverance and gentleness (1 Timothy 6:9–11).

This number ten Key to Success is: **Beware of the love of money**. Notice that this scripture does not say, as some have misinterpreted it, that money is evil. It does not tell us to avoid having money. It says that those who *want to get rich* are vulnerable to many temptations and desires that can bring on their ruin. It says that *the love of money* is a root of all sorts of evil. It warns us that the love of money has caused many people to stray from the Lord, the true source of wealth and blessings, in pursuit of money, which has brought them all sorts of sorrow as a result.

Notice also that this scripture does not say that *God* will punish us, bring us to sorrow, or bring on our ruin. It says that the temptations and desires to which we yield will lead us to ruin. By straying from the Lord, we lose access to his guidance, counsel, and protection and therefore come to ruin. In other words, we become vulnerable in ways in which we were not vulnerable while we were walking with him.

Look at these additional scriptures that warn us not to focus our energies on pursuing or acquiring wealth:

> Do not weary yourself to gain wealth,
> Cease from your consideration of it.
> When you set your eyes on it, it is gone.
> For wealth certainly makes itself wings
> Like an eagle that flies toward the heavens
>   (Proverbs 23:4–5).

> A faithful man will abound with blessings,
> But he who makes haste to be rich will not go
>   unpunished (Proverbs 28:20).

> A man with an evil eye hastens after wealth
> And does not know that want will come upon him
>   (Proverbs 28:22).

In chapter 2, which explained the importance of trusting in God, we looked at part of Jesus' Sermon on the Mount in Matthew 6:31–34. Let's return to that passage and look at some of the verses that precede it.

> Do not store up for yourselves treasures on earth, where moth and rust destroy, and where thieves break in and steal. But store up for yourselves treasures in heaven, where neither moth nor rust destroys, and where thieves do not break in or steal; for where your treasure is, there your heart will be also (Matthew 6:19–21).

Notice in these verses that it is expected that we *will* acquire wealth and treasures. The thing about them that affects us positively or negatively is *where we store them*. If we keep them all for ourselves (store them on earth), our focus will be on ourselves and on the things of earth. The danger is that we will become selfish, greedy people and will miss out on God's best for us. And remember, we can't take any of it with us when we die. All of it stays here. None of it is ours any longer at that point. Jesus illustrates that truth in a parable about a rich, greedy man who dies:

> And He told them a parable, saying, "The land of a rich man was very productive. And he began reasoning to himself, saying, 'What shall I do, since I have no place to store my crops?' Then he said, 'This is what I will do: I will tear down my barns and build larger ones, and there I will store all my grain and my goods. And I will say to my soul, "Soul, you have many goods laid up for many years to come; take your ease, eat, drink and be merry."' But God said to him, 'You fool! This very night your soul is required of you; and now who will own what you have prepared?' So is the man who

stores up treasure for himself, and is not rich toward God" (Luke 12:16–21).

While it is not possible to take any of our wealth with us to heaven, it *is* possible to send some of it on ahead. That is what Matthew 6:20 means when it says that we can store up treasures *for ourselves in heaven.* And how can we do that? We can do it by giving to God and by giving to the poor as we discussed in chapter 9, "Handle Money Wisely."

Mark 10 contains an interesting story about a rich young man who came to Jesus and asked what he must do to inherit eternal life. In the first part of Jesus' answer, he quoted from the Ten Commandments. But the young man was not fully satisfied with Jesus' answer. He believed that he had kept those commandments, yet he still didn't feel as if he possessed eternal life. Then Jesus gave him the rest of the answer:

> Looking at him, Jesus felt a love for him and said to him, "One thing you lack: go and sell all you possess and give to the poor, and you will have treasure in heaven; and come, follow Me." But at these words he was saddened, and he went away grieving, for he was one who owned much property (Mark 10:21–22).

Many people misunderstand the message of this passage. The message is that the way to inherit eternal life is to follow Jesus. The message is to get rid of anything that prevents us from following him. That young man's obstacle was the large amount of property that he owned and was responsible for.

The scriptures tell us that Jesus felt a love for that young man. We can therefore be absolutely certain that the action Jesus told him to take was in the young man's best interest.

Jesus was, in fact, personally inviting that young man to become one of his disciples, just as he had personally invited Peter, Andrew, James, John, and others. And what a missed opportunity it was for that young man!

Let me paraphrase and amplify a little on what Jesus said to help bring out its meaning. Jesus was saying,

> The one thing you must do to inherit eternal life is to come and follow me. I invite you to be one of my disciples. But I know that the large amount of property that you own is an obstacle to your being able to do that. You can't be traveling with me and simultaneously be overseeing your buildings, fields, vineyards, flocks, herds, and servants. So here is the way that you can follow me and still retain the value of these things for your life in eternity: transfer their worth to an account in your name in heaven. You can do that by selling them and giving the proceeds to the poor. Then you will have treasure in heaven, you will be free from the responsibility of overseeing those things, and you can come and be my disciple on a full-time basis. I love you, and I am not trying to impoverish you. Instead, I am trying to make you rich in heaven, where it really counts.

What an offer from the Lord! But Mark 10:22 says that the young man was unwilling to give up ownership of his possessions. It says that he was saddened and went away grieved. He missed the opportunity of a lifetime—the opportunity to be Jesus' disciple and to also be rich in heaven—because it was more important to him to be rich on earth.

Returning to the Sermon on the Mount, we hear Jesus saying:

> No one can serve two masters; for either he will hate
> the one and love the other, or he will be devoted to
> one and despise the other. You cannot serve God and
> wealth (Matthew 6:24).

A key word in this verse is *serve*. When we focus on wealth as an end in itself, we can easily fall into servitude to it. We can easily become a slave to greed and covetousness. The Lord does not want us to fall into that trap.

Another danger of pursuing wealth is that in pursuing it, our lives can become unfruitful in the things of God. In Luke 8 Jesus tells a parable about a man who went out and sowed seeds, intending that they grow and bear a crop. Let's focus on just one aspect of that parable. Verse 7 says:

> Other seed fell among the thorns; and the thorns grew
> up with it and choked it out (Luke 8:7).

When Jesus' disciples asked him to explain what the parable meant, Jesus told them that the seed is the word of God. The word of God is spoken to people so that they can hear it, plant it in their hearts, act on it, and produce fruit in their lives that will further God's kingdom. In Jesus' explanation of the meaning of this verse, he said:

> The seed which fell among the thorns, these are the
> ones who have heard, and as they go on their way they
> are choked with worries and riches and pleasures of
> this life, and bring no fruit to maturity (Luke 8:14).

Let us be careful not to let greed and the pursuit of wealth hinder us from fulfilling God's highest purposes for us.

Is being poor the preventative to greed? No, it is not. A person can be poor and still be greedy—excessively desiring to acquire money and possessions. If someone is poor, it may simply mean that up to now he has been unsuccessful in his pursuit of wealth.

Is it bad to be rich? No, it is not. In fact, if we faithfully conform to the Keys to Success that God lays out for us, it will be difficult to keep from becoming rich. The secret is to pursue God, not wealth; to love God, not money; to look to God as our source, not to any wealth which we may acquire. As the book of Hebrews says:

> Make sure that your character is free from the love of money, being content with what you have; for He Himself has said, "I will never desert you, nor will I ever forsake you," so that we confidently say,
> "The Lord is My helper, I will not be afraid.
> What will man do to me?" (Hebrews 13:5–6)

As we close this chapter, consider these words of the Apostle Paul:

> I know how to get along with humble means, and I also know how to live in prosperity; in any and every circumstance I have learned the secret of being filled and going hungry, both of having abundance and suffering need (Philippians 4:12).

And what does Paul say that this secret is?

> I can do all things through Him who strengthens me (Philippians 4:13).

PLAN OF ACTION

Let us be on the lookout for indications of greed, self-centeredness, and the love of money in our businesses, our careers, and our personal lives. One way to do this is to ask ourselves to what extent is our focus on serving God and to what extent is it on acquiring wealth. To the degree that we love money, we are in danger. We must repent of such an attitude, ask God's forgiveness, and ask him to help us reset our focus onto the things that are the most important to him.

Then we should seek ways to transfer some of our earthly possessions into a heavenly bank account in our name, an account that we can draw upon later.

11

AVOID PERSONAL PITFALLS

In chapters 1 through 9, we discussed positive Keys to Success that encourage us to do specific things that will increase our number of successes in business, our careers, and our personal lives. Chapter 10 warned us to beware of the love of money. This chapter warns us to: **Avoid personal pitfalls**. Falling into a pitfall can cancel some or all of our previous progress and, in the worst case, can literally destroy us. For this reason, we should take very seriously these warnings. There are many temptations that are of a serious enough nature to be potential pitfalls for us. We will address three:

- illegal activities
- adultery
- alcohol and intoxicants

ILLEGAL ACTIVITIES

In the first chapter of the book of Proverbs, immediately following the introduction, there is a warning from God. The warning is that other people may try to entice us to join them in doing something that we know we should not do. God then tells us that we must, for our own good, refuse to participate in such activities.

> My son, if sinners entice you,
> Do not consent.

> If they say, "Come with us,
> Let us lie in wait for blood,
> Let us ambush the innocent without cause;
> Let us swallow them alive like Sheol,
> Even whole, as those who go down to the pit;
> We will find all kinds of precious wealth,
> We will fill our houses with spoil;
> Throw in your lot with us,
> We shall all have one purse" (Proverbs 1:10–14).

The example given here is the invitation to join a group that will be ambushing and murdering innocent people to rob them without leaving any witnesses. This is clearly something that we know we should not be doing. Hopefully our *integrity*, which we discussed in chapter 5, will keep us from joining them. The *enticement* to join them is three-fold. First, there is the possibility that we will become rich: "We will fill our houses with spoil." Second, we will belong, share, and be a part of a profitable group. "We shall all have one purse." Third, there is the implication that the activity is risk-free and that there will never be any penalty to pay; in other words, we will get away with it.

Should we decide to join in? To phrase the question in a different way: Is it OK to do things that we know we should not be doing so that we can "belong" and make big money? The answer from God, of course, is a resounding *no*, for the text continues by saying:

> My son, do not walk in the way with them.
> Keep your feet from their path,
> For their feet run to evil
> And they hasten to shed blood.
> Indeed, it is useless to spread the baited net
> In the sight of any bird;
> But they lie in wait for their own blood;

> They ambush their own lives.
> So are the ways of everyone who gains by violence;
> It takes away the life of its possessors
> > (Proverbs 1:15–19).

There is a big flaw in the line of reasoning that the tempters have presented. By their own admission they are sneaks, murderers, and robbers toward everyone else. They then ask us to believe that they will be completely different toward us—honorable, harmless, and generous. We must not believe them!

The Lord loves us as a father loves a son, and his warning is clear in verse 10:

> My son, if sinners entice you,
> Do not consent.

as well as in verse 15:

> My son, do not walk in the way with them.
> Keep your feet from their path.

In modern parlance, God says, "Just say no!"

In verses 16 to 19 God plainly tells us that such people cannot be trusted. They only want to use us to further their own gains. The Lord compares their enticing words to an almost invisible net that a trapper uses to snare birds as they carelessly fly toward the bait, unaware of the danger. The Lord warns us that we can lose everything we have, including our very lives, through being enticed into doing what we know we should not do.

ADULTERY

There is a joke that when Moses came down from Mount Sinai with the Ten Commandments, he announced, "I have some good news, and I have some bad news. The good news is that there are only ten. The bad news is that adultery is included." The next major pitfall is that people may try to entice us into committing adultery.

Picture yourself as the naive young man described in the following passage in Proverbs 7. He can't believe his good fortune. As he is wandering aimlessly one evening, he is approached by a woman who is dressed very sensually. She offers him a night of beautiful, exciting, unrestrained sex. The only drawback is that she is married, but since her husband is out of town and should be gone for at least several more days, there is no risk.

> For at the window of my house
> I looked out through my lattice,
> And I saw among the naive,
> And discerned among the youths
> A young man lacking sense,
> Passing through the street near her corner;
> And he takes the way to her house,
> In the twilight, in the evening,
> In the middle of the night and in the darkness.
> And behold, a woman comes to meet him,
> Dressed as a harlot and cunning of heart.
> She is boisterous and rebellious,
> Her feet do not remain at home;
> She is now in the streets, now in the squares,
> And lurks by every corner.
> So she seizes him and kisses him
> And with a brazen face she says to him:
> "I was due to offer peace offerings;

Today I have paid my vows.
Therefore I have come out to meet you,
To seek your presence earnestly, and I have found
    you.
I have spread my couch with coverings,
With colored linens of Egypt.
I have sprinkled my bed
With myrrh, aloes and cinnamon.
Come, let us drink our fill of love until morning;
Let us delight ourselves with caresses.
For my husband is not at home,
He has gone on a long journey;
He has taken a bag of money with him,
At the full moon he will come home."
With her many persuasions she entices him;
With her flattering lips she seduces him.
Suddenly he follows her (Proverbs 7:6–22a).

Let's review the situation.

- The naive young man doesn't have anything to do. He is just wandering around with time on his hands.
- He is approached by a sexy woman who comes up, grabs him, and kisses him passionately. She implies that this is just an introductory sample of what is waiting for him. He likes it and stays for more.
- She flatters him by saying, "I have come out to meet you, to seek your presence earnestly, and I have found you." He accepts her flattery. The book of Proverbs calls him naive because he sees the upside of the situation, but he does not see the downside. He continues to listen to

her. By now, he really wants to be talked into this.

- She continues by describing in detail her bedroom and what the night will be like. She assures him that there is no danger, no down-side, no risk.
- He's completely sold on the idea and follows the woman.

What has this young man failed to notice or deliberately refused to consider in making his final decision? There are two key things. First, he assumed that nobody else would know, and therefore he would not be caught. But someone else did know what he was doing, for the text begins, "I looked out through my lattice and I saw..." Second, the penalty in the Old Testament law is death for both of them if they are caught.

> If there is a man who commits adultery with another man's wife, one who commits adultery with his friend's wife, the adulterer and the adulteress shall surely be put to death. (Leviticus 20:10).

Picking back up with the narrative:

> Suddenly he follows her
> As an ox goes to the slaughter,
> Or as one in fetters to the discipline of a fool,
> Until an arrow pierces through his liver;
> As a bird hastens to the snare,
> So he does not know that it will cost him his life.
> Now therefore, my sons, listen to me,
> And pay attention to the words of my mouth.
> Do not let your heart turn aside to her ways,
> Do not stray into her paths.

> For many are the victims she has cast down,
> And numerous are all her slain.
> Her house is the way to Sheol,
> Descending to the chambers of death
> (Proverbs 7:22–27).

Note that once again the Lord speaks as to a beloved son (verse 24). He states plainly that the enticement to commit adultery is a trap. Whether or not we know it, whether or not we admit it, this trap can destroy us.

> So he does not know that it will cost him his life (Proverbs 7:23c).

What is the solution? It is simple—total avoidance.

> Do not let your heart turn aside to her ways,
> Do not stray into her paths (Proverbs 7:25).

There is one more verse with a very clear warning against committing adultery.

> The one who commits adultery with a woman is
>   lacking sense;
> He who would destroy himself does it
>   (Proverbs 6:32).

ALCOHOL AND INTOXICANTS

The Bible does not say, "Never drink beer, wine, or other alcoholic beverages." But it is very clear that there are two thresholds of drinking which, if exceeded, endanger us. The first threshold is that of getting drunk.

> Wine is a mocker, strong drink a brawler,
> And whoever is intoxicated by it is not wise
>   (Proverbs 20:1).

> And do not get drunk with wine, for that is
>   dissipation (Ephesians 5:18a).

The second threshold is that of regular heavy drinking.

> Do not be with heavy drinkers of wine,
> Or with gluttonous eaters of meat;
> For the heavy drinker and the glutton will come to
>   poverty,
> And drowsiness will clothe one with rags (Proverbs
>   23:20–21).

Later in the same chapter of Proverbs, we see described a heavy drinker who progresses to a drunken stupor, passes out, and wakes up only to start looking for another drink.

> Who has woe? Who has sorrow?
> Who has contentions? Who has complaining?
> Who has wounds without cause?
> Who has redness of eyes?
> Those who linger long over wine,
> Those who go to taste mixed wine.
> Do not look on the wine when it is red,
> When it sparkles in the cup,
> When it goes down smoothly;
> At the last it bites like a serpent
> And stings like a viper.
> Your eyes will see strange things
> And your mind will utter perverse things.
> And you will be like one who lies down in the middle
>   of the sea,
> Or like one who lies down on the top of a mast.

> "They struck me, but I did not become ill;
> They beat me, but I did not know it
> When shall I awake?
> I will seek another drink" (Proverbs 23:29–35).

It is easy to see that these same warnings apply to the use of recreational drugs. The Lord wants us to be successful. Let us not let alcohol or other intoxicants sidetrack us.

> He who loves pleasure will become a poor man;
> He who loves wine and oil will not become rich
>   (Proverbs 21:17).

PLAN OF ACTION

For this chapter, the plan of action is very simple:

- We must not participate in illegal activities. If we're doing it now, we must cease.
- We must not commit adultery. If we're doing it now, we must cease.
- We must not drink heavily nor get drunk. If we're doing it now, we must cease.

If we have genuinely tried to stop these things and have been unable, we should seek wise counsel to help us. The Lord does not want any of these things to have mastery over us.

12

PRAY CONTINUALLY

Our twelfth and final Key to Success is: **Pray continually**. Without practicing this key, we will never be able to consistently adhere to the others. In this chapter we will look briefly at a number of aspects of prayer:

- Prayer lets us communicate with God.
- Pray without ceasing.
- Pray with thanksgiving.
- Pray about everything.
- Pray according to God's will.
- Pray for where we live and work.
- Pray for those in authority over us.
- Prayer has hindrances.
- Pray with an enlarged vision.

It is through effective prayer that we request and receive the resources we need from God for our daily lives and for when we are facing difficult situations. These resources include every kind of help—help that only God himself can provide. And *he will provide* for us in answer to our prayers, because he loves us and he has committed himself to help us as we cooperate with him.

PRAYER LETS US COMMUNICATE WITH GOD

Very simply, prayer is *communication with God*. Our role in prayer can take many forms including confession, repentance, petition, thanksgiving, and praise. Let me compare communicating with God to communicating with my wife. When I communicate with my wife, the only real prerequisites are that we be able to hear each other and respond to each other. We can talk about any subject whether we're face-to-face; side-by-side while driving in the car; nearby, but out of sight such as when she's in the kitchen and I'm in the den; or long-distance by phone. If I can hear her and she can hear me, we can have live, personal communication. Prayer is just like that. It is live, personal communication between God and us. The only prerequisites are that he hears us, and we hear him. There is no required formula or format for this communication.

When my wife and I see each other after a day at work, our first few words are mostly just a greeting.

"Hi. How was your day?"

"Busy. How was yours?"

"OK. Anything special happen today?"

It's almost like saying, "Testing: one, two, three," into a microphone to verify that the system is turned on and working. Are you there? Are you available for conversation? Can we talk now? Sometimes one of us is too tired or still too preoccupied with the events of the day to talk. At times like that, we postpone meaningful conversations until later in the evening. Most days, though, we begin right away talking about what has happened during the day— accomplishments, frustrations, things that were interesting or funny or eventful to us, or news items. We talk about anything that we want to share as well as anything we think the other might want to know. As we talk, we often reveal things about ourselves by telling what we thought or how we felt or how we responded to something that happened during the day. One of us may describe a problem or a decision we're facing and ask for the other's insights or advice. Only a small percentage of our conversation is in the form of requests such as, "Could you pick up some milk and bread on your way home tomorrow?" or, "I need you to..." Very often one of us asks the other, "Can I help you with that?" or, "Can I do anything for you?"

Our relationship with God can be like that. It can include frequent personal conversations with him. It includes us revealing ourselves to him—what we've been doing, what we've been thinking, the problems and decisions we're facing, asking for his help, and offering to be used to help him. And it includes God revealing himself to us—what he's doing, what he's planning, the situations he's working in, how he views our situation, the things we can be doing for him. This is one of the best ways to get to know him better.

Psalm 103 is a very descriptive passage about the Lord. It is worth reading regularly. Verse 7 says:

> He made known His ways to Moses,
> His acts to the sons of Israel (Psalm 103:7).

I do not want my relationship with the Lord to be limited to being an observer: merely seeing or hearing about his *acts*. I want to know his *ways*. I want to know *him*. I want to participate with him in the things that he is doing. That kind of relationship develops through communicating with him in prayer.

PRAY WITHOUT CEASING

In his first letter to the Thessalonians, the Apostle Paul wrote, "Pray without ceasing" (1 Thessalonians 5:17).

He reiterated that message in three other letters:

> With all prayer and petition pray at all times in the
>   Spirit (Ephesians 6:18a).

> But in everything by prayer and supplication with
>   thanksgiving let your requests be made known to
>   God (Philippians 4:6b).

> [Be] devoted to prayer (Romans 12:12c).

Just what does pray *without ceasing* mean? I believe it means keeping the lines of communication with God so open that we are always ready to speak to him and hear from him. I believe that it also means being diligent and persistent in our praying. It means staying alert. For instance, when I know that a particular person needs help from the Lord, I want to pray for him or her every time the Lord brings that one to my mind, whether that's monthly, weekly, daily, or often during the day. *Praying without ceasing is being dedicated to prayer.*

God desires that we fellowship with him continually. He desires that we be continually aware of his presence with us and of his constant accessibility to us. We can experience these things as we function throughout the day whether we are working, playing, eating, talking to friends, or whatever we may be doing. *Praying without ceasing is continual fellowship with God.*

PRAY WITH THANKSGIVING

Philippians 4:6, which we just read, says we should pray *with thanksgiving.* Colossians 4:2 says, "Devote yourselves to prayer, keeping alert in it with an attitude of thanksgiving."

Thanksgiving is an important element of the way we pray because it reminds us of who God is and how much he has been doing for us. It helps us remember how good God is, how he has blessed us, and how he has answered so many of our other prayers. When we focus on him and his goodness, it is easier to have faith that he will help us with our current needs.

God, not our prayers, is the source of our strength and our supply. Our prayers are simply the way that we express our needs to him. When we are able to pray with thanksgiving, keeping our focus upon him, it is easier to receive and recognize the answers to our prayers. Receiving and recognizing answers to our prayers give us even more reasons to shower thanksgiving on him who answers our prayers.

PRAY ABOUT EVERYTHING

Philippians 4:6 also says we should pray *in everything*: in every problem, in every situation, in every circumstance. God has placed no bounds on the parameters of our prayers. There are no disqualified subjects of prayer. He has never said, "That circumstance is too trivial for you to bother me with. Handle it yourself." He may on occasion say to us, "I have already told you how to handle that. Now do it."

He has never said, as I often have, "That problem is too difficult for me to solve." Rather, the Lord himself asks Abraham, "Is anything too difficult for the Lord?" (Genesis 18:14a).

The prophet Jeremiah declared,

> "Ah Lord God! Behold, You have made the heavens and the earth by Your great power and by Your outstretched arm! Nothing is too difficult for You" (Jeremiah 32:17).

In the same chapter, the Lord responded,

> "Behold, I am the Lord, the God of all flesh; is anything too difficult for Me?" (Jeremiah 32:27).

God invites us to pray about everything: ourselves, our families, our friends, our church, our business, our career, our finances, our health. Our successes will be greater if we seek his counsel in prayer, especially before we make major decisions. Let us continually avail ourselves of the counsel and help of the God who created and sustains the universe. Let us pray about everything.

PRAY ACCORDING TO GOD'S WILL

The scripture passage that has probably had the greatest impact on the way that I present my requests to God in prayer is this one:

> This is the confidence which we have before Him, that, if we ask anything according to His will, He hears us. And if we know that He hears us in whatever we ask, we know that we have the requests which we have asked from Him (1 John 5:14–15).

There are two conditions—two *if-clauses*—in these verses. The significance of these two if-clauses is very clear to me because I often used if-clauses when I designed or analyzed computer software for various jobs. The significance of an if-clause is this: To achieve the desired result—that we have the requests that we have asked from him—we must satisfy the preceding if-clauses. The first if-clause in the passage is this: "If we ask anything according to His will..." God tells us that before we petition him with our request, we should first determine his will related to the matter at hand. In other words, a prayer asking God to reveal his will to us—followed by our acceptance of his answer—should precede our petitions. It is only after we have aligned our will with his will that we should present our petitions to him.

The second "if-clause" is having confidence that he has heard us: "If we know that He hears us in whatever we ask..." Someone may want to know how many times to pray about a thing—once, seven times, or until the answer is received? I believe this scripture says we should pray until we have confidence that he has heard us.

When we have met the two conditions, the end result is that we know that we have the requests that we have asked from him. To summarize, our process for praying according to 1 John 5:14–15 is to determine his will, pray according to his will, and then receive what we have asked from him.

PRAY FOR WHERE WE LIVE AND WORK

The theme verse for this book is Jeremiah 29:11, in which the Lord says that his plans for us are plans for our welfare. In this context, "welfare" includes our health, happiness, success, and prosperity. Jeremiah 29:11 is an excerpt from a letter that God directed the prophet to send to the Jewish exiles in Babylon. In Jeremiah 29:4, God said they were living in Babylon because he sent them there. In verses 5 and 6, he told them to establish homes and businesses there, to raise families, to multiply and prosper. Then in verse 7 he said:

> Seek the welfare of the city where I have sent you into exile, and pray to the Lord on its behalf; for in its welfare you will have welfare (Jeremiah 29:7).

A lesson for us from these verses is that we too should regularly pray on behalf of the place where we live—our city, county, state, and nation. We should also pray for the place where we work—our company and its customers—for as these prosper, we too will prosper.

PRAY FOR THOSE IN AUTHORITY OVER US

In 1 Timothy Paul wrote:

> First of all, then, I urge that entreaties and prayers, petitions and thanksgivings, be made on behalf of all men, for kings and all who are in authority, so that we may lead a tranquil and quiet life in all godliness and dignity (1 Timothy 2:1–2).

When we pray, we should include in our prayers those in high positions in the federal government. They set the tone for our nation through the laws and regulations they write and through the ways they interpret and enforce those laws and regulations. They decide how to allocate federal taxes and how to spend federal tax revenues.

We should pray for our state and local officials. They make decisions that affect our schools, law enforcement, fire protection, and roads. They make decisions that determine how friendly and attractive our communities are to the business growth that can provide new and better jobs.

We should pray for our managers and supervisors where we work, for they set the tone of our work environment. They are also responsible in large part for bringing in new customers so that the business can grow and prosper.

PRAYER HAS HINDRANCES

Any good user manual includes troubleshooting instructions. Suppose I bought a hair dryer and when I plugged it in, it did not work. The troubleshooting instructions might tell me to do the following:

- Check to see that it is plugged in properly.
- Check to see that the switch is on.
- Reset the built-in circuit breaker.
- If it still doesn't work, plug a lamp or other appliance into the wall socket to verify that power is available.

The manufacturer instructs the new owner how to overcome some of the common hindrances to using the new hair dryer.

In the same way, God provides troubleshooting instructions for our prayer lives. There are a number of common hindrances that can keep us from receiving the things we pray for.

Perhaps we have simply been assuming that God knows what we need and that we therefore don't need to ask him for it. The book of James says that we may not be getting what we need from God because we have not asked him:

> You do not have because you do not ask (James 4:2b).

We need to explicitly ask for the things we need from the Lord. Jesus confirmed the importance of asking:

> Ask, and it will be given to you; seek, and you will find; knock, and it will be opened to you. For everyone who asks receives, and he who seeks finds, and to him who knocks it will be opened (Matthew 7:7–8).

Another possibility is that we have asked, but with wrong motives:

> You ask and do not receive, because you ask with
> wrong motives, so that you may spend it on your plea-
> sures (James 4:3).

We need to examine our motives and be certain that they
are proper in God's sight.

James wrote that another possibility is that we doubt
God's ability, his willingness, or his readiness to give us the
things we need.

> But if any of you lacks wisdom, let him ask of God,
> who gives to all generously and without reproach, and
> it will be given to him. But he must ask in faith without
> any doubting, for the one who doubts is like the surf of
> the sea, driven and tossed by the wind. For that man
> ought not to expect that he will receive anything from
> the Lord, being a double-minded man, unstable in all
> his ways (James 1:5–8).

Jesus confirmed doubt as a hindrance when he said:

> Therefore I say to you, all things for which you pray
> and ask, believe that you have received them, and they
> will be granted you (Mark 11:24).

Let us defeat any doubt that attempts to prevent us from
trusting in the goodness of God.

In this same passage of Mark, Jesus said that unforgive-
ness will hinder our prayers.

> Whenever you stand praying, forgive, if you have
> anything against anyone, so that your Father who is
> in heaven will also forgive you your transgressions
> (Mark 11:25).

Let us be quick to forgive others, so that our prayers will not be hindered.

The Apostle John wrote that keeping God's commandments—specifically believing in Jesus and loving one another—is important to receiving answers to our prayers.

> Beloved, if our heart does not condemn us, we have confidence before God; and whatever we ask we receive from Him, because we keep His commandments and do the things that are pleasing in His sight (1 John 3:21–22).

Jesus said the same thing this way:

> If you abide in Me, and My words abide in you, ask whatever you wish, and it will be done for you (John 15:7).

The Apostle Peter told those of us who are married that our prayers can be hindered when we are not treating our spouses as God intends.

> You husbands in the same way, live with your wives in an understanding way, as with someone weaker, since she is a woman; and show her honor as a fellow heir of the grace of life, so that your prayers will not be hindered (1 Peter 3:7).

PRAY WITH AN ENLARGED VISION

The Apostle Paul wrote that God is able to do infinitely more than we will ever be able to even think of asking.

> Now to Him who is able to do far more abundantly beyond all that we ask or think (Ephesians 3:20a).

The incident in my own life that forever convinced me of this truth occurred in the late summer of 1968, less than a year after I had become a Christian. I had just completed the electrical engineering course work for my doctorate and had finished studying for my qualifying examination. The qualifying examination at that time was a week-long, take-home test covering the areas of electrical engineering in which each student had specialized. For me these were control systems, digital simulation of systems, and random variables and probability. I, along with the other doctoral students taking the exam, picked up my test on Monday morning and had until Friday afternoon to complete it.

When I arrived back at my apartment and began to read through the test, I was stunned! There were fourteen problems, each of which would take two to three hours to solve—*if I knew how to solve them*. I knew how to solve six of the problems. I had never been taught, independently studied, or even seen anything like the other eight! It was obvious to me that six out of fourteen would not be a passing grade.

I began doing what I could and solved the six problems. "What do I do now?" I wondered. I stared at the first unsolved problem for a few minutes. I didn't have a clue how to begin solving it. Then I did what so many other people do when they are facing a desperate situation: I prayed! I don't remember my exact words. My prayer was probably as simple as, "Lord, I don't know how to work this problem. Please help me." When I finished praying, I suddenly knew how to solve the problem! It still took a couple of hours to do the work, but I knew how to do it.

My score was now seven out of fourteen. That was better, but it was still not a passing grade. I thought, "If God helped me with that one, maybe he will help me with the next one."

I read through the problem, reconfirming that I had no idea how to even get started. Then I prayed, and God suddenly planted in my mind an understanding of how to work that problem!

That's how the rest of the week went. I would read a problem and confirm that there was absolutely no way that I could solve it on my own. Then I would pray and suddenly I knew how to solve it. By the time I had to turn in my test, I had fully solved twelve of the fourteen problems, and had partially solved the other two. I had passed, thanks to God answering the prayers of a desperate person.

By the end of that week—one of the most difficult weeks I had ever faced—I was forever convinced that:

- God is.
- He is accessible to us when we need him.
- He is gracious to help us.
- He is really smart—much smarter than I am.
- He is a much better engineer than anyone ever gives him credit for being.
- It's great to have him on your side.

SUMMARY

Let us summarize what we have studied about prayer:

- Prayer lets us communicate with God.
- Pray without ceasing.
- Pray with thanksgiving.
- Pray about everything.
- Pray according to God's will.
- Pray for where we live and work.
- Pray for those in authority over us.

- Prayer has hindrances.
- Pray with an enlarged vision.

Plan of Action

Our prayers—or the lack of them—can have a major impact on our successes in our businesses, careers, and personal lives. We should plan our prayer strategy and then execute our plan.

An organized way to begin is by assessing our schedule for each day of the week. We can then choose a time or times when we will give top priority to spending time with God, getting to know him better and praying for our own needs and for the needs of others. I recommend starting modestly, praying for ten minutes each day, perhaps on the way to work. During this time, we can pray for our families, our companies, and our tasks for the day. I also recommend praying for a few minutes on the way home, thanking God for hearing us and helping us throughout the day.

Later we can add short prayers for specific purposes throughout the day. Examples include asking for guidance in making a decision, asking for wisdom about what to do and say in an upcoming meeting, asking for help in completing a specific task, and asking for favor with a particular customer. We should be sure to thank him for each time he helps us. God is good. He wants to help us. Jesus told us to *ask and we would receive.*

CONCLUSION

The main purpose of this book has been to proclaim from the Bible that **God wants us to succeed!** The book has also described ways in which we may have been sabotaging the success that God wants to give us. The theme scripture has been, "For I know the plans that I have for you," declares the Lord, "plans for welfare and not for calamity to give you a future and a hope" (Jeremiah 29:11).

Each chapter presented one Key to Success along with a recommended Plan of Action. The twelve keys we have covered are:

1. Establish a personal relationship with God.
2. Trust in God.
3. Walk humbly with God.
4. Deal honestly and truthfully with others.
5. Maintain your integrity.
6. Heed wise counsel.
7. Be diligent.
8. Treat everyone with respect.
9. Handle money wisely.
10. Beware of the love of money.
11. Avoid personal pitfalls.
12. Pray continually.

Before putting this book away, I recommend going back and identifying those Keys to Success that would make the most immediate positive impact on your own business, career, and personal life. Re-read the Plan of Action associated with each of them. Then consolidate those individual Plans of Action into your own composite Plan of Action. Set a date to implement your plan. Then start the plan, be diligent in following the plan, and look to the Lord for your successes. Treat it as an adventure with God.

I challenge you to put these Keys to Success to the test. Be objective about it: document your successes so that you will be more aware of your progress. This will also help you build your trust in God.

After you have successfully followed your initial Plan of Action, gradually enlarge your plan to incorporate the other Keys to Success. Next, begin reading the book of Proverbs for yourself, being alert for whatever messages the Lord may have for you at that moment. You may discover answers to questions that you have. You may discover solutions to problems that you are facing. You may discover other items to incorporate into your Plan of Action. In this way, your adventure with God can continue.

We shall close with these words of the Apostle Paul, in which he so beautifully brings these Keys to Success together:

> Let love be without hypocrisy. Abhor what is evil; cling to what is good. Be devoted to one another in brotherly love; give preference to one another in honor; not lagging behind in diligence, fervent in spirit, serving the Lord; rejoicing in hope, persevering in tribulation, devoted to prayer, contributing to the needs of the saints, practicing hospitality.
>
> Bless those who persecute you; bless and do not curse. Rejoice with those who rejoice, and weep with those who weep. Be of the same mind toward one another; do not be haughty in mind, but associate

with the lowly. Do not be wise in your own estimation. Never pay back evil for evil to anyone. Respect what is right in the sight of all men. If possible, so far as it depends on you, be at peace with all men. Never take your own revenge, beloved, but leave room for the wrath of God, for it is written, "Vengeance is Mine, I will repay," says the Lord. "But if your enemy is hungry, feed him, and if he is thirsty, give him a drink; for in so doing you will heap burning coals on his head." Do not be overcome by evil, but overcome evil with good (Romans 12:9–21).

ENDNOTES

INTRODUCTION

1. Matthew 25:21 (author's paraphrase)
2. John 14:2-3 (author's paraphrase)
3. John 17:24 (author's paraphrase)

CHAPTER 1

1. 1 Corinthians 15:3-4

CHAPTER 3

1.   Kathryn Spinks, *Mother Teresa* (San Francisco CA: HarperSanFrancisco, 1997)

CHAPTER 5

1.   Douglas G. Brinkley, *The Unfinished Presidency: Jimmy Carter's Journey to the Nobel Peace Prize* (New York NY: Penguin Books, 1999)

SCRIPTURE INDEX

OLD TESTAMENT

NEW TESTAMENT

ABOUT THE AUTHOR

Eugene H. Lowe has three degrees in electrical engineering: a doctorate from the Georgia Institute of Technology (1970), a master's degree from the University of Southern California (1967), and a bachelor's degree from Louisiana Tech University (1965). Dr. Lowe has nearly forty years of experience in the high-tech world of systems engineering. His thorough and analytical approach to his work and life influences his writing and research. He has worked on projects for the United States Air Force, Army, and Navy while employed by corporations that support the United States government.

Gene was raised in the liturgical tradition of the Episcopal Church. In college he met Brenda, a Southern Baptist girl, now his wife of forty-five years, and they have one son. Gene committed his life to the Lord in 1967, and both he and his wife were baptized with the Holy Spirit in 1971. That inaugurated a dynamic period of Bible study and personal growth that has continued to the present. Gene and Brenda have been members at various times of the Methodist Church, the Assemblies of God, and the Church of God.

Gene's relationship with the Lord is intimate and personal. He has a passion for knowing and fellowshipping with the Lord, for reading and understanding the Bible, and for worship through music whether alone, in small groups, or in church. This book is an outgrowth of his study of the book of Proverbs while he was seeking practical information about God's way to conduct business.

Gene has a gift for recognizing the most significant ideas in important subjects and then presenting those ideas in a clear, inspirational, and easily understandable manner. He says, "My end objective is much more than merely presenting biblical truth. It is to present biblical truth in such a way that it inspires the reader to take appropriate action while simultaneously drawing him or her toward a closer relationship with God."

IF YOU'RE A FAN OF THIS BOOK, PLEASE TELL OTHERS...

- Write about *Heaven's Success Secrets* on your blog, Twitter, MySpace, and Facebook page.

- Suggest *Heaven's Success Secrets* to friends.

- When you're in a bookstore, ask them if they carry the book. The book is available through all major distributors so any bookstore that does not have *Heaven's Success Secrets* in stock can easily order it.

- Write a positive review of *Heaven's Success Secrets* on www.amazon.com.

- Send my publisher, HigherLife Publishing, suggestions on Web sites, conferences, and events you know of where this book could be offered.

- Purchase additional copies to give away as gifts.

CONNECT WITH ME...

If you would like to have Dr. Lowe speak at your church, conduct a seminar, do a media interview, or sign books, you may contact him at 407-739-0516 or email him at GeneLowe@TheHolySpiritatWorkinYou.com.

You may also contact my publisher directly to learn more about *Heaven's Success Secrets*:

HigherLife Development Services
400 Fontana Circle
Building 1 – Suite 105
Oviedo, Florida 32765
Phone: (407) 563-4806
Email: info@ahigherlife.com